knitgrrl

LEARN TO KNIT
WITH **15** FUN
AND FUNKY
PROJECTS

PHOTOGRAPHY BY SHANNON FAGAN,
CHRISTINE OKEY, AND TAMAS JAKAB
ILLUSTRATIONS BY KATHLEEN JACQUES

Shannon Okey

SENIOR ACQUISITIONS EDITOR: **Julie Mazur**
EDITOR: **Linda Hetzer**
DESIGNER: **Margo Mooney**
SENIOR PRODUCTION MANAGER: **Ellen Greene**

First published in 2005 by Watson-Guptill Publications,
Nielsen Business Media, a division of The Nielsen Company
770 Broadway, New York, NY 10003
www.watsonguptill.com

Library of Congress Control Number: 2005927913

ISBN: 0-8230-2618-3

Printed in China

First printing, 2005

2 3 4 5 6 7 8 9 / 13 12 11 10 09 08

For Tamas, Anezka, and Spike

acknowledgments

My thanks to the designers, who so generously shared their time and talent, to the yarn companies who supplied materials, to photographer Shannon Fagan and to all the models who endured an extra-long photo shoot to make the designs look fabulous. But there are many others behind the scenes who made this book what it is....

My mother, Christine Okey, took all the instructional photos. My partner, Tamas Jakab, edited them so my hands don't look like living cat scratches. My "furry children," Anezka and Spike, were always there to step on my keyboard, run off with a ball of yarn, or just sleep patiently while I wrote. Illustrator Kathleen Jacques also draws the coolest web comic ever. Tech editor Kristi Porter made sure the patterns were correct, and kept me sane in the process. Extra-big hugs to my fairy knitmother Jillian Moreno, Amy Singer of Knitty.com, and Lucy Lee of Mind's Eye Yarns in Cambridge, Massachusetts, for everything they do. Someday I will have a yarn room as big as Jillian's, and when I do, I will have to open a store like Lucy's to get rid of it all!

contents

introduction
WHY KNIT? — 6

chapter 1
WHAT DO YOU NEED? — 8

Yarn — 9
QUIZ: What kind of yarn girl are you? — 11
Needles and other tools — 14
Reading patterns — 16

chapter 2
KEEPING YOU IN STITCHES — 18

Holding your needles and yarn — 19
Casting on — 20
How to knit — 22
Creating knit fabric — 25
Joining new yarn — 26
Binding off — 27
Weaving in ends — 28
Seaming — 28
Uh-oh! Two common mistakes — 29
Love your swatch! — 30

chapter 3
GETTING STARTED — 32

Rocker-Girl Wristlets — 33
Friendship Scarf — 34
Boombox Bag — 36
DIY: Host a knitting party! — 39

chapter 4
SHAPING IT UP — 40

How to increase — 41
How to decrease — 43
Faux Fur Stole — 46
Kitty Dim Sum — 48
Stripey Scarf — 51

chapter 5
GETTING AROUND — 52

Working with circular needles — 53
Ponytail Roll-Brim Hat — 54
Heartfelt Roll-Brim Hat — 56
D.I.Y. Leg Warmers — 58
DIY: Make your own stitch markers — 61

chapter 6
SEEING DOUBLE — 62

How to use double-pointed needles — 63
Knitting with more than one color — 64
Music Player Cozy — 66
Soda Cozy — 69
Text-Messaging Mittens — 70
DIY: Make your own knitter's hand salve — 73

chapter 7
I FELT IT WAS TIME — 74

Felting — 75
Blocking — 77
Downtown Messenger Bag — 78
Lacy Double-Diamond Scarf — 80

chapter 8
MAKIN' IT FANCY — 82

Pom-poms — 83
I-cord — 84
Cables — 85
Embroidery — 86
Nakiska Alpine Headband — 88

chapter 9
AND STILL MORE... — 90

Caring for your hand-knit items — 91
Help! Where to get answers — 92
Places to go, things to read — 93
Meet the designers — 95

Index — 96

INTRODUCTION
why knit?

Why knit? This is a question many non-knitters will ask you, sometimes over and over. After all, you can go to the mall and buy a hat in five minutes, so why spend five hours to knit your own? That, however, is exactly the point. Anyone can buy a hat; not everyone can *make* one. When you make your own, you can knit it with whatever colors, materials, and decoration you want. It's your choice and you are in control.

Knitting is amazing because you only have to learn a few simple skills for quick results, and you can do it anytime, anywhere. Imagine wearing a unique hat, sweater, or scarf every day that you knitted yourself. It's a very satisfying feeling—you're always in style when you create your own style!

You may have noticed that DIY (do-it-yourself) clothing and accessories are all the rage lately, but the DIY trend isn't really that new. It can be traced back 10–15 years to a number of sources, the most influential of which was Riot Grrl (which inspired *KnitGrrl*'s title). Riot Grrl was a loosely knit international community of musicians, 'zine makers, community activists, and others who did amazing things in the early 1990s. They were tired of the same old music, books, clothes, and magazines…so they made their own! Thousands of young women and men were encouraged to start their own projects, from record labels to magazines, and more. Riot Grrl is still around today, although its activities have shifted names and format.

Like all the other DIY gurus before you, don't worry if you don't know what you're doing at first, because you'll soon figure it out. Knitting has been around for thousands of years—even the ancient Egyptians knit socks! Be confident and the rest will come. Soon you'll be able to teach everyone you know how to knit. If you do come from a family of knitters, you're already halfway there. Try asking your mom, grandma, or aunts for help—chances are at least one of them will be able to show you the basics.

If you don't know anyone who knits, don't worry—you'll soon know not only the local yarn store's owner by name, but probably most of her customers, too! If your local yarn store (abbreviated "LYS" by many knitting websites) offers group lessons, make an effort to meet other knitters of your level. They're good friends to have around as you learn the craft. Odds are, if you can't figure something out, one of them already has, or you can try to work it out together.

Forming a knitting group that meets regularly is another great way to get help as you learn. You'll spend time with your friends, catch up on all the latest news, and be crafty, too. I wrote this book with *my* knitting friends' help. One pattern designer I see every Tuesday at knitting group, a few I've met in person once or twice, and some I know only online—but we all have knitting in common.

You can also take part in online knitting communities. Knitting blogs (weblogs, a type of regularly updated journal-style website) and online knitting forums are the perfect ways to find help on your latest project, learn about new yarns or patterns, and trade knitting materials. Some of the most popular ones are listed in the guide at the back of the book. And be sure to check out this book's website, www.knitgrrl.com. We're here to help you learn, even if the nearest yarn store is miles away!

Happy knitting!

web

Check out www.knitgrrl.com to ask questions, post photos of your projects, chat with other knitters, and much more!

CeLeBriTY KniTTers

Imagine you're a famous musician or actress and you have lots of time to kill on the tour bus, or between movie scenes. Perhaps this is why so many celebrities have taken up knitting in recent years. On a recent movie set, Catherine Zeta-Jones sewed "Personally knit by CZJ" labels inside the ponchos she knitted as gifts. Julia Roberts, Madonna, Sandra Bullock, Cameron Diaz, Tyra Banks, Sarah Jessica Parker, Debra Messing, and Julianne Moore have all been spotted with needles

in hand. Hollywood knitters tend to shop at La Knitterie Parisienne, or at Edith Eig's or Suss Cousins' shops—their favorite places for yarn in Los Angeles.

Unfortunately, the most famous male knitter, Russell Crowe, doesn't even knit. He earned his knitting reputation thanks to a publicity photo that shows him holding knitting needles. Maybe one of you would be willing to teach him and make the rumor come true?

WHAT DO YOU NEED?

1

Take a minute to learn about yarn, needles, and the other tools knitters use. They aren't particularly complicated, and knowing about them will make everything so much easier.

yarn

Knitting is all about the yarn. Choosing the right yarn for a project isn't difficult; it just requires a little planning. Do you want a soft and fluffy decorative scarf? Eyelash yarn could be right for the job. What about an extra-warm scarf for the middle of winter? Stick to wool. Don't worry—even though it seems there are thousands of yarn types, they all boil down to a few simple categories.

Yarn is classified by thickness, or **weight.** The thinnest, or lightest, yarn is called **super fine,** while the thickest, or heaviest, yarn is **super bulky.** Different patterns call for yarns of different weights. For example, for a chunky winter sweater you'll probably want a heavier-weight yarn.

The Craft Yarn Council of America has developed a chart to classify yarn by weight. Here's our version of the chart below.

Most patterns will tell you exactly what kind of yarn to use, so the only thing you need to choose is the color. But if you're feeling adventurous, you can decide to use a different kind of yarn—the sky's the limit! If you do want to change the yarn, it's easiest to stay close to the same yarn weight if you can. (See page 31 for tips on substituting yarn.) As you become a more experienced knitter, picking the right yarn becomes second nature. Many knitters will adjust a pattern they like just to experiment with a new kind of yarn. You can, too. Try fancy yarns, like eyelash, or use railroad ribbon as decoration in the first few inches of a hat. You'll never be bored if you make every pattern your own!

THE CRAFT YARN COUNCIL OF AMERICA'S STANDARD YARN WEIGHT SYSTEM

YARN WEIGHT CATEGORY	SYMBOL	TYPES OF YARN	HOW MANY STITCHES MAKE 4 INCHES OF KNITTED FABRIC?	RECOMMENDED NEEDLE SIZES (US)	RECOMMENDED NEEDLE SIZES (METRIC)
Super fine	1 SUPER FINE	Sock, fingering, baby	27–32 sts	1–3	2.25–3.25 mm
Fine	2 FINE	Sport, baby	23–26 sts	3–5	3.25–3.75 mm
Light	3 LIGHT	DK, light worsted	21–24 sts	5–7	3.75–4.5 mm
Medium	4 MEDIUM	Worsted, afghan, aran	16–20 sts	7–9	4.5–5.5 mm
Bulky	5 BULKY	Chunky, craft, rug	12–15 sts	9–11	5.5–8 mm
Super bulky	6 SUPER BULKY	Bulky, roving	6–11 sts	11 and larger	8 mm and larger

This chart shows you how yarn is put into categories by weight. If you like a pattern but want to switch the yarn, you can usually pick another one in the same weight category. You'll learn more about substituting yarn on page 31.

reading a yarn label

Most yarn comes wrapped in a label with lots of important information on it. In addition to the basics—the manufacturer's name, yarn name, and yarn color (or sometimes a color number)—the yarn label will tell you the following:

Fiber content. This is what the yarn is made of—wool, cotton, nylon, for example. If the yarn is a blend, it will give you the percentage of each fiber.

Dye lot number. When yarn is dyed a color, it is given a dye lot number. If you are making a large item that calls for several balls of yarn, be sure you buy balls that all have the same dye lot number—this means they were dyed together, in the same batch. Yarn with a different number may be slightly different.

Weight and quantity. The weight will be given in ounces or grams; the quantity will be given in yards or meters.

Gauge and needle size. The gauge is the number of stitches and rows in a 4-inch square, using the recommended size needles. (More about this on page 30!)

Care instructions. To take care of your knitted items, you need to know what the manufacturer suggests for washing and drying.

Many yarn manufacturers have started using standard symbols on their labels. This is a new standard that is still being adopted. The symbols below show, from left to right, the yarn's weight, the recommended gauge for knitting needles (shown as a swatch, with the needle size laid diagonally across), and the same thing for crochet hooks. The last two show care instructions—the water temperature for washing, and the type of dryer cycle (this one is for a normal cycle; a delicate cycle would have a line under the circle).

what kind of yarn girl are you?

Having a tough time picking what yarn to use? With so many beautiful yarns available today, it's hardly surprising. Try this quiz and learn what type of yarn girl you are.

1 GETTING READY IN THE MORNING TAKES:

a Less than 15 minutes, as long as you can find your favorite jeans.

b At least 30 minutes. You need a shower to wake up!

c More than an hour. You need 15 minutes for makeup alone.

d You're not sure. It's hard to see the clock when you're up before dawn!

2 YOUR FASHION STYLE COULD BE BEST DESCRIBED AS:

a Comfy.

b Preppy.

c Cheerful.

d Glam.

3 YOUR FAVORITE COLORS ARE:

a Dark colors like black, navy, and gray. They're easiest to keep clean!

b Earth tones and neutrals.

c Bright pinks, purples, and other pastels.

d Is glitter a color?

4 YOU'VE BEEN ASKED TO STAR IN A MOVIE! WHICH ROLE WOULD YOU WANT?

a The star athlete who scores the winning goal.

b The smart, cool investigator who solves the crime.

c The quirky artist who becomes a foreign spy.

d The beautiful girl-next-door who rises to superstardom.

5 YOUR FAVORITE SHOES ARE:

a Sneakers, what else?

b Ballet flats. They're classy and trendy, too.

c Your purple flip-flops with flowers on top.

d Strappy heels—they make you feel like a rock star!

6 IT'S A RAINY, GRAY SUNDAY. WHICH DVD DO YOU REACH FOR?

a A feel-good movie.

b A cute chick-flick.

c An indie or foreign movie.

d An action adventure.

7 WHAT KIND OF MAKEUP DO YOU WEAR?

a Nothing! You like to go au natural.

b Just lip gloss.

c Depends on the day! You like to experiment.

d Blush, eye shadow, lip gloss— the works!

8 YOUR DREAM CAREER IS:

a Scientist.

b Writer.

c Artist.

d Movie star.

9 WHAT'S YOUR FAVORITE DESSERT?

a Homemade chocolate chip cookies.

b Apple pie with ice cream.

c Peanut-butter brownies.

d Chocolate mousse.

10 AS A KID, YOU USED TO:

a Be a tomboy.

b Like to make your mom and dad happy.

c Love to make a mess.

d Have lots of tantrums!

scoring

MOSTLY As – **You're practical and like comfort. Check out worsted wool and natural fibers.**

MOSTLY Bs – **You're into the classics with a twist. Try bright-colored tweeds or alpaca boucle.**

MOSTLY Cs – **You're lively and a little offbeat. Take a look at railroad yarns and unique handpainted fibers.**

MOSTLY Ds – **You're the life of the party and you like to attract attention. Try eyelash, metallic, and other fancy yarns.**

CHOOSING COLORS

Knitting is not only about personal choice in terms of style, but in colors, too. If you don't want your scarf to be green, you don't have to knit it that way! Since color is probably the single most distinguishing feature of clothes and accessories, it's worth putting some thought into what colors are right for you.

Choosing the right color yarn is more an art than a science. But like any art, it's a question of understanding the materials. You wouldn't try to paint without knowing how to hold the brush, would you?

Say you want a yellow scarf. What color yellow? Sunflower yellow, or mustard yellow? Or what if you want a scarf that has yellow and blue stripes? You've just doubled the number of color choices. It's enough to make you put down your yarn and run away screaming!

You may think that two particular colors of yarn will go together well until you hold them next to each other and they "feel" wrong. In contrast, colors you thought would never look right side-by-side do. Here's how you can simplify the process right off the bat and make good color decisions.

The entire spectrum of colors visible to the human eye can be broken down and simplified into a "color wheel," like the one shown opposite. Designers often use color wheels to pick colors because it helps narrow down the choices.

Yarn comes in a mouth-watering range of colors, textures, and thicknesses.

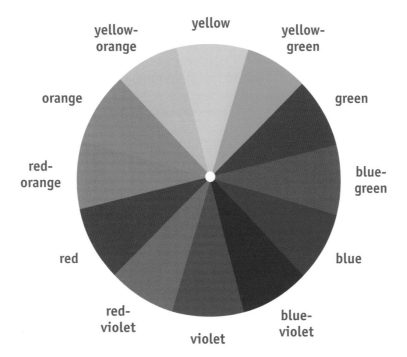

yellow-orange · yellow · yellow-green · orange · green · red-orange · blue-green · red · blue · red-violet · blue-violet · violet

Colors that are generally across from each other on the wheel (such as violet and green) can be very striking when used together. This is why violet eye shadow looks so good on green-eyed people.

Tone is how dark or light a color is, or how much black it contains. Pure yellow is light and bright, but if you mix in some black it becomes more mustard-colored. Keep your colors in the same general tone range for a more "even" effect. Bright blue and bright yellow may look good together; bright blue and mustard yellow probably won't.

Tint is the amount of white a color contains. Pure blue is considerably different from blue with a little white added. Mixing dark- and light-colored yarns can create interesting effects. "Shadow knitting" and other advanced techniques use this principle to make darker parts of the knitting recede from your view, highlighting the lighter parts and making them pop out. If you mix dark and light yarns, remember

that the lightest color will always stand out the most—even if they're all just different shades of the same color.

Experiment with your own favorite colors to see which combinations you prefer. Put together items you already have to see how the colors look, and then buy corresponding yarns. Do you always wear your teal-colored shirt with dark denim jeans? Try teal and navy together in a scarf. Do you like the way your red cereal bowl looks on top of an orange saucer? Knit a hat that combines the two. Whatever you try, you're the designer—it's a You Original!

needles and other tools

After yarn, the most important item you will use to knit is knitting needles. There are many kinds to choose from, some more common than others. Most needles you'll see these days are made from plastic, wood, bamboo, or metal.

Straight needles are probably what you think of when someone says "knitting needles"—long, smooth needles that are pointy on one end, with a knob on the other.

Circular needles are two needles connected by a flexible plastic cord. Circulars have lots of advantages over straight needles. They keep the project's entire weight evenly balanced in the center, which keeps your wrists from supporting all that yarn. (You'd be surprised how quickly the ounces of yarn add up!) Your hands, wrists, and elbows are held in a more natural position, and some knitters swear that they can knit faster with circular needles. Circular needles can be used for almost any pattern, even if it is designed for straights. Here's how: Every time you reach the end of a row, turn your knitting around and start going across the row again, just as you would with straight needles. Try both circular and straight needles and see which you prefer.

Double-pointed needles, or **DPNs,** are straight and pointy at both ends. DPNs can be used to knit small tubes, like the Soda Cozy on page 69, or to finish off tight circles, such as the top of the Ponytail Roll-Brim Hat on page 54.

Needles come in various sizes, and patterns and needle packages will usually list them in both U.S. and metric sizes (see the conversion chart, above right). So which size needles should you buy, assuming you haven't inherited a bagful from someone in your family? Well, you can buy each different size as you need them. If you're knitting a scarf this week that requires size 10s, buy 10s. Next week, if you need 5s for something else…buy those, too. The only problem with this is that it becomes very expensive very quickly. Murphy's Knitter's Law says you will always need a needle size you don't have as soon as all the yarn stores have closed for the weekend. (Of course, if you're always knitting patterns that use the same size needles, you can get along with just a few pairs!)

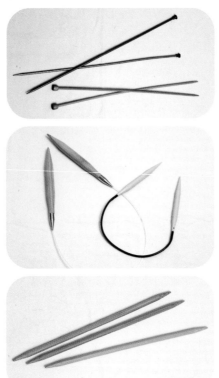

NEEDLE SIZES (US)		NEEDLE SIZES (METRIC)
3	—	3.25 mm
4	—	3.5 mm
5	—	3.75 mm
6	—	4 mm
7	—	4.5 mm
8	—	5 mm
9	—	5.5 mm
10	—	6 mm
10.5	—	6.5 mm
11	—	8 mm
13	—	9 mm
15	—	10 mm
17	—	12.75 mm
19	—	15 mm
35	—	19 mm
50	—	25 mm

Fortunately, there's a simple answer to the question of what size needles to buy: the Denise needle system. This is a kit that you can use to make any number of different size circular needles. You just pick out a pair of needle tips in whatever size you need and twist them onto the end of a flexible cord. If you need to switch needle size, just twist off the needle tips and twist on another size.

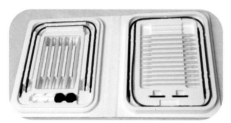

OTHER TOOLS

Here's a list of other knitting tools you'll need. They can be found at almost any crafts store and at all good yarn stores.

Tapestry needles (sometimes called **yarn needles**) are a must-have in every knitter's bag. They look like oversized sewing needles with an eye large enough to thread yarn through, and blunt tips. Tapestry needles are used to weave in loose ends after you've changed balls of yarn and/or after you've finished a project. You will need a tapestry needle for every pattern in this book, and probably every pattern you'll ever knit! They are the fastest and easiest way to weave in ends when you're finished knitting.

You'll need a small pair of **scissors** to cut yarn. You probably already have scissors, but it helps to have a small pair you can carry with you in your knitting bag. Mine fold up!

Stitch markers help you keep track of how many stitches or rows you've done. (See page 61 for instructions on making your own.)

A **row counter** (sometimes called a *kacha-kacha*, for the sound it makes) is used to keep track of how many rows you've knitted. Every time you come to the end of a row, you twist the side or click the button and the number goes up by one.

Crochet hooks aren't just used in crochet. They're good to have when you drop a stitch or need to pull yarn through something that's too small for your fingers. Of course, if you already know how to crochet, you can use it to add an extra dimension to your knitting, too!

Stitch holders look like huge safety pins. If you need to hold some stitches in reserve, you can slip them onto the holder and keep them separate while you continue knitting elsewhere.

They come in handy, but are not necessary. If you just need to hold a few stitches temporarily, you can slip them onto an extra circular needle.

reading patterns

Most patterns will give certain information at the beginning for you to read through before you actually start to knit, from what yarn was used for the item shown, to which needle sizes and other tools you'll need. It's important to read through a pattern thoroughly before you start, to make sure you have all the materials and to understand how the finished item will be put together.

In this book, each pattern gives the names of the pattern and designer, the skills you need to do that pattern, the finished measurements and/or size, the materials needed (both yarn and tools), the pattern gauge (more on that later), the pattern itself, and any special directions for finishing up.

If a pattern uses two colors of yarn, they are indicated by **MC** (main color) and **CC** (contrasting color). If a pattern uses more than two colors, they are indicated as **Color 1**, **Color 2**, and so on.

A pair of **asterisks** (* *) means that whatever directions are between them should be repeated. For example, "*Knit 3, purl 1* to end of row" means that you should knit 3 stitches and then purl 1, over and over, until you reach the end of the row.

We've written our pattern directions almost entirely in plain English, but most other patterns are written with special abbreviations (like **k** for **knit**).

tip

Always read through a pattern before you begin and look up any terms you are not familiar with.

Check out the abbreviations chart opposite for a list of the most common ones. Keep it handy for when you need help deciphering other patterns.

new to knitting?

If you're just starting to knit, you might want to begin with the first project in the book, Rocker-Girl Wristlets on page 33. You can make these quickly and without having to worry about using the right size needles or type of yarn.

As you read through the book, you'll see that each chapter introduces new skills. The skills are listed at the beginning of each project so it's easy to see what you need to know. It's a good idea to check out any new skill before starting the pattern—flip to the page that teaches that skill, read through the directions, look at the step-by-step photos, and even practice with a spare piece of yarn. That way, you'll feel confident when you actually start working on your project.

knitting abbreviations

Most patterns use abbreviations rather than writing out every word. Although they may look like secret code, the abbreviations are really very simple. Here are some of the most common ones you'll see. Keep this page handy and use it as reference when you start working with other patterns.

* *	repeat directions between * * as many times as indicated
alt	alternate
approx	approximately
beg	begin[ning]
BO	bind off [cast off]
cab	cable
CC	contrasting color
cn	cable needle
CO	cast on
cont	continue[ing]
dec	decrease[ing]
DPN	double pointed needles[s]
foll	follow[s][ing]
g	grams
inc	increase[ing]
incl	including
inst	instructions
k	knit
k1fb	knit in the front and back of the next stitch (increase)
k tbl	knit through back of loop
k2tog	knit 2 stitches together (decrease)
m	meter[s]
MC	main color
m1	make 1 stitch (increase)
mm	millimeters
mult	multiple
opp	opposite

oz	ounce[s]
p	purl
p2tog	purl 2 together (decrease)
patt[s]	pattern[s]
psso	pass slipped stitch[es] over
rem	remaining
rep	repeat
rev St st	reverse stockinette stitch
RS	right side[s]
rnd[s]	round[s]
sc	single crochet
SKP	slip 1 stitch, knit 1 stitch, pass the slipped stitch over the knitted stitch (decrease)
SSK	slip 2 stitches as if to knit, knit 2 stitches together (decrease)
SSP	slip 2 stitches as if to purl, purl 2 together (decrease)
sl	slip
slp	slip 1 as if to purl
sl st	slip stitch
st[s]	stitch[es]
St st	stockinette stitch
tbl	through back of loop[s]
tog	together
WS	wrong side[s]
YO	yarn over
YO2	a yarn over with the yarn wrapped twice around the needle

keeping you in stitches

2

Ready to get started? This chapter will teach you all the stitch basics you need to know, from putting the yarn on your needles to removing it again!

holding your needles and yarn

In this book, all the photos demonstrate the "English," or "American," style of knitting. In this style, you hold the needles close to their tips. You use your dominant hand (the one you write with) to wrap the yarn around the needle. I'm right-handed, so I use my right hand to wrap. (Though this is hardly a strict rule—many lefties prefer to knit right-handed. If you're left-handed, try it both ways and use whichever you feel more comfortable with.)

Some people prefer the "Continental" style of knitting, which uses the non-dominant hand to wrap the yarn. There's also "combination" knitting, which combines the two. None of these styles is better than the other—use whichever is easier and faster for you. As long as you can make the stitches look the way they should, don't worry!

In the "English" or "American" style of knitting, you hold the needles close to their tips and use your dominant hand (the one you write with) to wrap the yarn around the needle.

tip

It takes time to get used to balancing needles and yarn. Don't grip the needles too tightly, or your hands will get tired almost immediately!

casting on

There are many ways to start your first row of knitting, called **casting on.** We'll show you the most common kind: the long-tail cast-on. Here you start with a slipknot as the first stitch, but it's not required. My own mom doesn't do the knot; she just skips it and starts with step 2.

1 Start by making a slipknot, as shown, and **tighten it slightly around the needle.**

tip

A trick of the trade: It takes three times as much yarn to cast on—or to knit across a row—than that row is wide. So if the scarf you're making is going to be 10 inches wide, pull out at least 30 inches of yarn before starting your cast on.

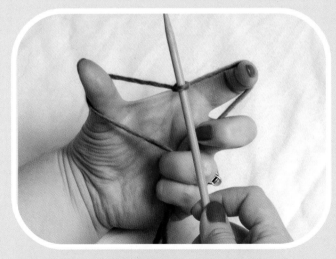

2 Hold the needle in your right hand. Grasp the two tails of yarn in your left hand. Wrap one tail around your left thumb and one around your left index finger, as shown. Use your other fingers to hold the yarn in place.

3 Point the needle down toward the base of your thumb and pick up the loop there.

4 Bring the loop up and around, then place the needle tip over and through the loop that's running around your index finger.

5 Bring the right loop through the center loop.

6 Release your thumb and index finger and pull down on the strands to tighten the first loop onto the needle.

Repeat steps 2–6 to cast on more stitches (your pattern will tell you how many). Your needle will move in a sort of sideways figure-8 as it rotates through the loops. Stop and count the stitches on your needle every once in a while until you have the right number.

tip

If you find you are casting on too tightly, use the next larger needle size. Then, once you've finished casting on your first row, slip the stitches back onto the correct size needle.

how to knit

Once you have your first row cast onto the needle, the next step is to start knitting. All knitting is made up of two stitches—really! There's the knit stitch, and the purl stitch. Let's examine the stitches as they're made, step-by-step.

THE KNIT STITCH

1 Put the needle through the stitch to the back of the work.

2 Wrap the yarn around the tip of the needle you pushed through, from back to front.

3 Pull the needle with the new yarn wrapped around it through to the front.

4 Slide the needle with the new stitch off to the right.

tip

Some patterns may refer to your "working yarn." This is the long strand of yarn that extends from the ball or skein you are using to your needle.

THE PURL STITCH

Purling gets a bad rap—it's not nearly as tough as some would have you believe. Purling is simply knitting done backwards and inside out.

1 Put the needle through the stitch to the front of the work.

2 Wrap the yarn around the needle you pushed through, from front to back.

3 Push the needle with the new yarn wrapped around it through to the back.

4 Slide the needle with the new stitch off to the right. Not so hard after all, right?

Continue knitting or purling every stitch on your needle, one after the other (if you're following a pattern, it will tell you what to do). As you go, the stitches will transfer from one needle to the other. When you've knit or purled all the stitches on your needle, you've finished one **row**. Then just swap the needles so the one holding the stitches is back in your non-dominant hand (for me, the left), and continue on the next row. If you're knitting in the round on circular needles, you won't need to switch hands—you'll just pass the stitch marker and keep going (for more on this, see page 53).

creating knit fabric

By combining knit and purl stitches in certain ways, you create different kinds of knit fabric. The three most basic types—and ones used throughout the patterns in this book—are called **garter** (sometimes called "garter stitch"), **stockinette**, and **reverse stockinette**. Most knitters don't consider these stitch patterns, a term reserved for more decorative work. You'll learn how to make decorative stitch patterns in the Heartfelt Roll-Brim Hat on page 56 by alternating knit and purl stitches in specific ways.

When knitted "flat" on straight needles, your knitted work has a front and a back (called the **right side** and **wrong side**, often abbreviated **RS** and **WS**). Every time you finish a row and switch your needles, you are switching from the front, or public, side to the back (or vice-versa). When you knit a tube on circular needles or DPNs, the wrong side is automatically made on the inside and you don't have to worry about switching hands.

GARTER STITCH

To make the garter stitch, all you do is knit every single stitch, in every row. Two rows of knitting create what's called a **ridge**. Some patterns written for garter stitch may ask you to count ridges instead of rows, because they're easier to track.

STOCKINETTE

If you knit each row on the right side of your work (the front) and purl each row on the wrong side (the back), you get what's called the stockinette stitch. Stockinette is probably what you think of when you hear "knitting"—a fabric made up of little V's lined up in rows.

reverse stockinette

If you flip the work over and look at the stockinette stitch from the back (or wrong side, where all the little purl bumps live), the pattern looks different. This is called reverse stockinette. Some yarns look more interesting on the bumpy purl side than they do on the right side, and the pattern will intentionally place the purl side on public view. You don't have to do anything differently to make reverse stockinette, but if it's meant to be shown, you'll weave in ends on the other side of the fabric when you're done.

joining new yarn

Most patterns you'll encounter use more than one ball of yarn. So what do you do when the first ball runs out? Easy—just join a new ball! Here's how. In these photos, the blue yarn is "new."

1 Leave a tail 3–4 inches long hanging from the old yarn. Take the new yarn and fold over the first 4 inches. Insert the needle into the next stitch as usual. Loop the new yarn over the needle.

2 Pull the needle through, just as you would for a normal knit stitch.

3 Complete the stitch with the new yarn by sliding it off the needle. Now just continue knitting using the new yarn.

4 For the next few stitches with the new yarn, you may need to hold onto both old and new yarn ends to keep your stitches from getting too sloppy. If they do get a little loose, you can give the two yarn ends a tug.

binding off

All good things must come to an end…otherwise you'll be knitting scarves forever with no finish line in sight! Time to learn to **bind off,** or finish, the knitting you've been working on. This is one instance where sloppiness will help you.

At the beginning of your last row, knit two stitches. Make your stitches very loose and sloppy! (Trust me—the tighter they are, the tougher it will be.) If you are using circular needles, as in these photos, start at the beginning of the last round.

1 Using the tip of your left needle, lift the second-to-last stitch over the last stitch.

Keep repeating these steps until there is only one stitch remaining on the left-hand needle. Cut your yarn, leaving a tail 6–8 inches long. Insert the tail through the last stitch and pull to tighten.

2 Drop the stitch off in the middle. Knit another stitch, then repeat steps 1–2 with those two stitches.

weaving in ends

When a project is done, you'll end up with "tails" of yarn hanging off your project. The way to get rid of them is to weave them into the wrong side of the knit fabric. This is called **weaving in ends.**

Thread one of the tails onto a tapestry needle. Then carefully weave it through an inch or two of stitches on the wrong side. In the photo below, you can see the blue yarn end woven through purl bumps, with extra sticking out so you can see where they're going. In real life, you would pull the yarn firmly and the yarn ends would disappear behind the bumps.

Since yarn ends come in pairs (one from the old ball, one from the new), you'll need to weave each end in separately. Weave the yarn end on the right into stitches to the left, and vice versa. This prevents a hole from appearing on the right side of the project.

This is how the tails look before you weave them in.

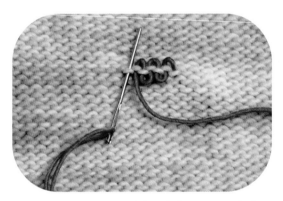

Weave the yarn ends in under the purl bumps.

seaming

Sometimes you'll make a project in pieces that then have to be sewn together (such as the Boombox Bag on page 36). **Seaming**, or **grafting**, is a way to join two pieces of knit fabric together. It's as easy as weaving in ends.

Place the two knitted pieces next to each other on a flat surface. Thread a tapestry needle with yarn, then use it to weave back and forth between stitches on either side.

uh-oh! two common mistakes

Probably the two most common mistakes any knitter makes are accidentally dropping stitches, and adding extra ones. (Not just beginners! Believe me, I've had my share of dropped stitches...as recently as yesterday!) But they're not disastrous, and they're easy to recover from.

TOO FEW STITCHES ON YOUR NEEDLE

Sometimes a stitch falls off of your needle while you're knitting. This is called **dropping a stitch.** If you drop a stitch and realize it right away, it's easy to put the end of the needle back into the stitch—just be careful not to twist it in the wrong direction when you put it on. But what if you dropped a stitch several rows ago? That's almost as easy to fix, but you'll need a crochet hook or tapestry needle. The photos below show you what to do.

TOO MANY STITCHES ON YOUR NEEDLE

Sometimes you might accidentally add a stitch by doing something called a **yarn over,** or **YO.** A yarn over can also be done on purpose—it creates a decorative hole (or "eyelet") in the knitted fabric, and is also a way to add a stitch. The yarn over gets added when you wrap your yarn around the needle more than once when knitting a stitch—you might do this by accident when you are first learning. If you realize you've accidentally done this, there are two ways to fix it. Either drop the stitch on the next row by sliding it off your needle, or (if you're still on the same row) "backspace"! Slip completed stitches from your right needle back onto the left until you reach the yarn over, then slide it off the end of the needle. Now just return the other stitches back to your right needle. Bye-bye, yarn over!

It's a good idea to count stitches every once in a while as you work through a pattern, to keep track of how many you have.

1 To find the dropped stitch, look for a skip in the row of regular stitches that looks like a ladder rung.

2 Insert your crochet hook into the front of the dropped stitch loop, and put the hook around the next "rung" of the ladder. Pull the rung forward through the stitch loop. In the photo, the blue yarn is acting as the dropped stitch so you can clearly see how the hook is used to pull stitches through.

If your stitch was dropped several rows ago, keep pulling "rungs" through the stitch, moving up the "ladder" until you can finally put the stitch back on the knitting needle. Depending on how tightly you knit, it may be difficult to pick up the stitch the farther it's dropped, but have patience.

love your swatch!

If there's one rule in knitting, it's this: Love your swatch. And I'm not talking about wristwatches! A **swatch** is a sample piece of knitting made before you start your actual project, made with the same needles, stitches, and yarn. It's used to measure your **gauge,** which is the number of stitches per inch of knitting. You need to make sure your gauge matches the gauge listed in the pattern. Imagine how frustrating it would be to spend weeks, or even months, knitting something that was the wrong size when finished! Swatching helps you see if you're using the right size needles. It also comes in handy when you want to use a different yarn than what's listed in the pattern. To test your gauge before trying a new pattern, do this:

Using the same size needles listed in the pattern and the yarn you plan to knit with, cast on 20 stitches. If the pattern uses more than one stitch, choose the most common stitch for your swatch. For example, if you're knitting a scarf with a garter stitch edge and stockinette center, knit the swatch in stockinette.

Knit back and forth until your swatch is a square, at least 4 inches long by 4 inches wide—any smaller and you won't be able to measure the gauge properly. If you're using a very thick yarn, less than 20 stitches

tip

Don't swatch when you're tired, angry, or nervous. Even the best knitters knit differently under those circumstances—and besides, knitting should be fun!

These swatches are all 20 stitches wide by 25 rows long. The one on the far left was knitted with size 5 needles, the one in the middle with size 8 needles, and the one on the right with size 11 needles.

may be enough. Bind off the stitches and place the swatch on a flat surface. Careful! This is knitting, not yoga. You don't want to stretch it and distort your measurements.

Lay a ruler across the swatch and count the number of stitches from side to side in 1 inch of knitting. Do this in a couple of places to double check. Does it match your pattern's gauge? If the pattern gauge is 2.5 stitches per inch, and you have 3 stitches per inch, your finished project will be too small. Change to the next larger size needles and try your swatch again. If you have only 2 stitches per inch, it will be too large. Change to the next smaller needle size and do your swatch again. You can unravel the one you just made and reuse the yarn. After you've found the right needle size for the yarn and pattern, start your project! (Note: Some patterns will write the gauge per 4 inches of knitting. To find out what the gauge is for 1 inch, just divide the number they give you by 4.)

A slight variation is okay for most projects; it will usually even out over the long run. More than one stitch in either direction is definitely too much. For items that are fitted, like a hat or mittens, make sure your swatch gauge isn't off by more than half a stitch. For something less exact, like a scarf, it's okay to be off by a little more, but keep in mind that your finished object may not look exactly like the photo.

If you want to use a different yarn than what's called for in the pattern, here's what to do. Let's say you want to use a different brand of yarn to make a hat. The yarn specified in the pattern has a gauge of 4 stitches per inch (or 16 stitches per 4 inches). But the label on the yarn you want to use says it knits at 5 stitches per inch (or 20 stitches per 4 inches). Is it okay? Look back at the chart on page 9. Both yarns are considered #4 Medium (worsted) yarns, so that's

web

Got a problem you don't know how to solve? Visit www.knitgrrl.com for help!

good. But you may need to use a larger sized needle to make your yarn knit at the desired 4 stitches per inch. Try a swatch and see. When you are first learning, needle size affects how your yarn will knit more than almost anything else.

In my opinion, Denise needles (see page 15) are the best needles for swatching. If you've knit a few inches and discover your gauge is not correct, switch the needle tips for the next size up or down and just keep knitting until you find the right one! It's one of many reasons I recommend them to knitters who are only just starting to develop their swatching "sixth sense."

Some knitters don't reuse the yarn from their swatches. Instead, they keep them until they have enough to sew together for an afghan. Why not collect swatches with all your knitting friends and make a special gift for someone?

GETTING STARTED

3

This chapter gets you started with three simple patterns that don't look beginner-y. Believe it or not, soon you'll be wearing things you've knitted yourself!

rocker-girl wristlets

PATTERN BY SHANNON OKEY

skills casting on, knit stitch, binding off, weaving in ends, seaming

This is a great way to get your feet wet. Start by making wristlets in one solid color, like the pink one above. Later, as you learn more skills, try adding stripes! Specific yarn, needles, and gauge are not important here. I used leftover yarn with size 8 needles, but use whatever you have on hand.

materials

- Yarn scraps (at least 10 yards per wristlet, or a combination of colors)
- 1 pair straight needles (any size)
- Tapestry needle

gauge

- Approximately 3–5 stitches = 1 inch

pattern

(make 2, unless you want to wear it on only one wrist)

- Cast on 25 stitches.
- Knit in garter stitch (knit every row) until piece measures 1–3 inches long.
- Bind off.

finishing

Weave in loose ends. Stitch the sides together with a tapestry needle and try on.

For one-of-a-kind wristlets, sew on buttons or beads or use embroidery to add designs or initials! Most of these have been felted (see page 75).

friendship scarf

PATTERN BY GABRIELLE PETERSON

skills casting on, knit stitch, joining new yarn, using a stitch holder, binding off, weaving in ends, seaming

This is a fun project to knit with a friend. Each of you can make one "leg" of the scarf in the color of your choice, then stitch them together. It's an updated version of the old "friendship necklace," which is made up of two halves of a heart. Another cool thing is how this scarf is tied: You place the center of the "X" at the back of your neck, then tie together the first two pieces in front. On top of those, you tie the other two pieces. Voilà! There's less bulk at the back of your neck, but you're still toasty-warm in the front. When you've finished making one scarf, start on another one for your friend!

materials

- 2 skeins of Crystal Palace Fizz in different colors [100% polyester; 120 yds per 50g skein] (Colors used here: Denim and Fern)
- 2 skeins of Crystal Palace Splash in the same color [100% polyester; 85 yds per 100g skein] (Color used here: Picnic)
- 1 pair size 11 (8mm) straight needles
- Stitch holder
- Tapestry needle

gauge

- 16 stitches/16 rows = 4 inches in garter stitch

pattern (repeat 2 times, once for each half)

- With a strand of Splash, cast on 32 stitches.
- Work for 2 inches (8 rows) in garter stitch (knit each row).
- Next row: Knit 14 stitches, then bind off next 4 stitches. Knit remaining 14 stitches.
- Next row: Attach a single strand of Denim-colored Fizz (you'll now be working with 2 strands of yarn) and knit 14 stitches. (To learn how to attach new yarn, see page 26.) Transfer remaining stitches to stitch holder.
- Work remaining stitches on needle in garter stitch until piece reaches 20 inches in total length (including first 2 inches). Bind off.

finished measurements

Width at center: 8 inches
Total length: 40 inches

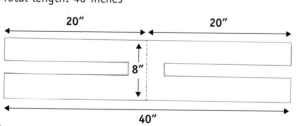

⑥ Transfer stitches from stitch holder to needle. Attach a single strand of Fern-colored Fizz (this piece should be a different color from the first "leg" you completed). Work the piece (with 2 strands of yarn—Splash and Fizz) in garter stitch until it reaches 20 inches in total length (including first 2 inches). Bind off.

finishing

First weave in any loose yarn ends. Then place the two pieces end to end, as shown, and sew them together with a tapestry needle and yarn.

To wear your scarf, tie the two bottom "legs" first. Then tie the other two pieces on top.

USING a STITCH HOLDER

Sometimes you need to move stitches to a stitch holder to "reserve" them while you do something else in the pattern. Moving stitches is easy.

1 Insert your stitch holder into the stitch on the needle that you want to move, as if you were purling.

2 Then pull it off the needle.

If you don't have a stitch holder, use a spare piece of yarn instead. Just thread a tapestry needle with the extra yarn and slip it through the stitches, as in step 1. Then ditch the needle and loosely tie the ends of the yarn together to keep the stitches in place.

3 Continue with as many stitches as you want to reserve.

4 Then just close the stitch holder.

When you're ready to put the stitches back on your needle, open the stitch holder and carefully slide them right back onto the needle.

boombox bag

PATTERN BY SHANNON OKEY

skills casting on, knit stitch, using a row counter, increasing (make 1; see page 41), binding off, weaving in ends, seaming, I-cord (optional)

O kay, okay, I'll admit it. I'm a child of the '80s. I actually remember the kids down the street breakdancing! Back then, it was cool to have the largest boombox possible...now it's cool to have the smallest music device. Go figure. This bag has built-in speakers, but you can also listen with headphones if you're not into the '80s thing.

measurements

Unfinished main panel: 10 x 15 inches
Finished purse: about 10 x 6 inches

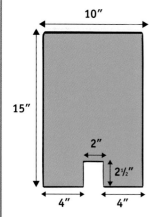

materials

- ⊚ 2 skeins of Brown Sheep Lamb's Pride Bulky [85% wool, 15% mohair; 125 yds per 113g skein] (Color used here: Kiwi)
- ⊚ 1 pair size 8 (5mm) straight needles
- ⊚ Row counter
- ⊚ ½ yard of cotton fabric to line bag
- ⊚ Sewing needle and thread to match yarn
- ⊚ Tapestry needle
- ⊚ Tiny portable speakers (optional)
- ⊚ 2 pieces of Velcro (plus craft glue, if the Velcro does not have a sticky back)

gauge

16 stitches/32 rows = 4 inches in garter stitch

pattern

Main panel:

- ⊚ Cast on 60 stitches.
- ⊚ Knit 30 rows.
- ⊚ Bind off first 10 stitches, then knit remainder of row.
- ⊚ Knit 18 rows.
- ⊚ Knit to where you previously bound off, then add 10 new stitches using the "make 1" method (see page 41).
- ⊚ Knit 30 rows.
- ⊚ Bind off all stitches.

Side panels (make 2):

- ⊚ Cast on 25 stitches.
- ⊚ Knit 20 rows.
- ⊚ Bind off all stitches.

Straps (make 2):

- ⊚ Cast on 7 stitches.
- ⊚ Knit every row until the piece is 10 inches long, then bind off.

[Note: You can also make I-cords for straps (see page 84), and felt them for an extra-sturdy handle (see page 75).]

more -->

tip

You can always swap circular needles for straight ones—that way you won't have to support the weight of the knitted piece with your hands and wrists. See page 14 for more about using circular needles.

finishing

1. Weave in any loose ends. Cut a rectangle of lining fabric 12 x 24 inches (as wide as the panel plus 1 inch on either side, and as long as the panel plus 1 inch on one end plus 8 inches for the pocket). With the lining fabric right side up, turn under the extra inch on the two long sides and one short side and press with an iron. Now fold under the extra 8 inches on the bottom and iron that flat, too.

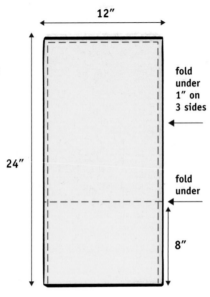

12"

24"

fold under 1" on 3 sides

fold under

8"

2. Place the lining fabric with the wrong side facing the inside of the knit panel. The end with the extra 8 inches folded under should be at the panel end with the notch (where you bound off while knitting).

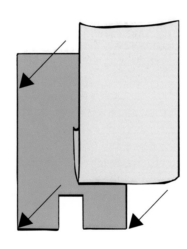

3. Using sewing thread, stitch the lining to the inside of the bag, following the outside edges first. Take your musical device (iPod, cassette player, etc.) and put it inside the cut-out notch. Stitch the lining around the device, creating a pocket. Be sure to leave enough room to easily remove it when needed!

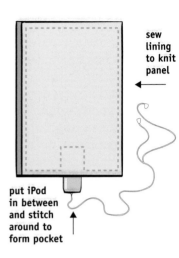

sew lining to knit panel

put iPod in between and stitch around to form pocket

4. Using yarn and a tapestry needle, graft the side panels and and straps into place.

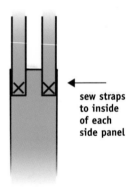

sew straps to inside of each side panel

5. Attach Velcro pieces to the back wall of the purse. Attach the corresponding pieces to the back of your speakers, using strong craft glue. Press play!

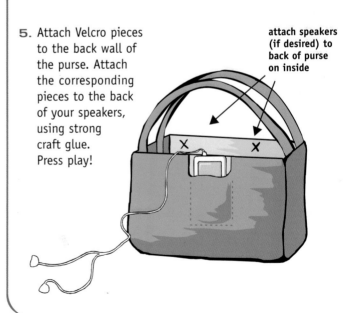

attach speakers (if desired) to back of purse on inside

host a knitting party!

Host a knitting party with these great favors, and soon you'll have plenty of knitting company.

Roll a handful of yarn into a very loose ball and place it in the bottom of the container (it will look like noodles). Insert the chopsticks. If you want to add name tags, cut a piece of paper into strips and write each guest's name on one strip, then tie it to the container handle with ribbon.

Your guests can use the chopsticks as basic knitting needles. Teach them how to cast on their "noodles" and knit garter stitch. Start with a small swatch, or maybe a narrow scarf. (Do you have cats? Try making the Kitty Dim Sum pattern on page 48.) Continue the Chinese theme by serving tea and fortune cookies.

FOR EACH FAVOR YOU WILL NEED:

- ◉ Approximately 100 yards of cream-colored yarn (a 200-yard skein will "serve" 2 people)
- ◉ One Chinese takeout container (ask your favorite restaurant!)
- ◉ Pair of chopsticks

SHAPING IT UP

4

Hats and sweater sleeves
don't magically become
larger and smaller in
just the right places.
The knitter (you!) has
to add or subtract
stitches— INCREASE
or DECREASE—in
order to shape them.

how to increase

There are two simple ways to add stitches as you knit, and both are used in the patterns in this book. The easiest way to add stitches is called **make 1** (often abbreviated as **m1**).

make 1

1 With your left finger, make a loop of yarn (twist it toward you).

2 Place the loop on the right needle.

3 There, you've added a stitch!

web

Need help increasing and decreasing? Check out www.knitgrrl.com.

KNIT THROUGH FRONT AND BACK LOOP

Another way to add a stitch is called **knit through front and back loop** (abbreviated as **k1fb**).
This is almost like a regular knit stitch.

1 Place your needle in the loop and wrap the yarn around, just like a knit stitch.

2 Pull the stitch through toward you, again as if you were knitting, but don't pull it off the needle yet.

3 Take your right needle and go around the left needle to the back of the loop you just knit through.

4 Place the needle through the back loop and wrap the yarn around it.

5 Pull it through (this part is a little awkward at first; you need to angle your hands a bit).

6 Slip both new stitches off the needle.

how to decrease

There are a few different ways to decrease stitches. Usually the first decreases you learn are **knit 2 together** and **purl 2 together**.

KNIT 2 TOGETHER

When you are on a knit row, one of the easiest ways to decrease is to **knit 2 together** (abbreviated as **k2tog**).

1 Place your right-hand needle through the next two stitches on the left needle knitwise (that is, from front to back).

2 Wrap the yarn around the needle, as for a normal knit stitch.

3 Pull the needle through and slide both stitches off.

tip

It's more difficult to do k2tog if your stitches are too tight. So if you're having a tough time doing this stitch, loosen up!

purl 2 together

To decrease when you are on a purl row, you **purl 2 together** (abbreviated as **p2tog**).

1 Place your right-hand needle through the next two stitches on the left needle purlwise (from back to front).

2 Wrap the yarn around the needle, as for a normal purl stitch.

3 Pull the needle through and slide both stitches off.

knit 2 together through back loop

Another way to decrease is **knit 2 stitches together through the back loop** (abbreviated as **k2tog tbl**). This creates a decrease that slants to the left.

1 Put the right-hand needle through the back loops of the next two stitches on the left-hand needle.

2 Wrap the yarn around as with a normal knit stitch.

3 Pull the wrap through and slide both stitches off.

SLIP, SLIP, KNIT

Slip, slip, knit (abbreviated as SSK) is another type of decrease that slants to the left.

1 "Slip" one stitch from the left needle to the right purlwise. To do this, insert the right-hand needle into the stitch, from right to left, and pull it off.

2 Slip a second stitch the same way.

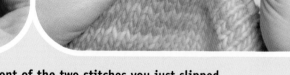

3 Now insert your left-hand needle into the front of the two stitches you just slipped. Wrap your yarn around the back and complete like a regular knit stitch.

faux fur stole

PATTERN BY MELISSA LIM

skills casting on, knit stitch, increasing (k1fb), decreasing (k2tog, k2tog tbl), weaving in ends

This faux fur stole will add an elegant and luxurious touch to anyone's wardrobe. It knits up very quickly on large needles, and any novelty fur yarn will work. Wear it with a fancy dress, or with a light sweater and your favorite jeans. Either way, you'll make a fashion statement!

finished measurements

Approximately 18 x 12–16 inches

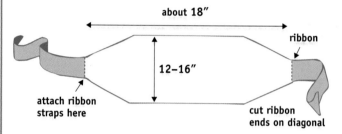

about 18"

ribbon

12–16"

attach ribbon straps here

cut ribbon ends on diagonal

materials

- 1 skein of Crystal Palace Splash [100% polyester; 85 yds per 100g ball] (Color used here: 7184 Silver Fox) [Note: You will need a second skein if you want to make your stole any larger.]
- 1 pair size 17 (12.75mm) straight needles
- 2 yards of satin ribbon in any color
- Sewing needle, and thread that matches your ribbon

gauge

10 stitches/10 rows = 4 inches in garter stitch

pattern

- Cast on 10 stitches.
- Row 1: Knit.
- Row 2: Knit 1, k1fb, knit to last 3 stitches, k1fb, knit 2.
- Repeat rows 1 and 2 until you have 36 stitches. Now work in garter stitch (knit every row) for 18 inches or desired length, ending with a wrong side (WS) row.
- Beginning on right side (RS), decrease as follows: Knit 2, k2tog, knit to last 4 stitches, k2tog tbl, knit 2.
- Continue working in garter stitch, but repeat decrease row every other row until you have 10 stitches left.
- Bind off these 10 stitches.

finishing

Weave in any loose ends. Then attach satin ribbon on either side of stole with a sewing needle and thread.

tip

The fabric this yarn creates is extremely stretchy. Try the stole around your shoulders as you knit until you reach a length that fits you.

SHORTER IS BETTER

We've tried to keep most pattern directions in plain English, but there are a few abbreviations that don't work well written out, including **k1fb** (knit through front and back loop), **k2tog** (knit 2 together), and **k2tog tbl** (knit 2 together through the back loop). Besides, getting used to these abbreviations will give you a head start when you use other patterns!

kitty dim sum

PATTERN BY JULIE FALATKO

skills casting on, knit stitch, purl stitch, decreasing (k2tog, SSK), using a row counter, binding off, weaving in ends, seaming

Cats love yarn, they love catnip, and they love clawing at knitted objects. These wonton and egg roll cat toys are perfect projects for using up extra yarn. If you don't have worsted weight yarn, don't fret. You can still follow the pattern, though you may end up with a slightly smaller or larger cat toy.

tip

Make sure the gauge is much tighter than normally required for the yarn you are using. With a normal gauge, the cat toys will be too loose and you will end up with catnip all over the floor. As long as you knit tightly with a smaller needle than usual, you'll be okay.

wonton

measurements

Unfinished: 5-inch square
Finished: 2½-inch triangular wonton shape

materials

- 1 skein of Brown Sheep Lamb's Pride [100% wool; 200 yds per 113g skein] (Color used here: Aran) [Note: You'll need 20 yards of yarn per wonton.]
- 1 pair size 5 (3.75mm) straight needles
- Row counter
- Tapestry needle
- Cotton balls, yarn scraps, and bits of fabric for stuffing
- Catnip (optional)

gauge

24 stitches/30 rows = 4 inches in stockinette stitch

pattern

- Cast on 30 stitches.
- Work in stockinette stitch (knit 1 row, purl 1 row) for 35 rows, or until you have a square (the piece should measure as tall as it is wide).
- Bind off all stitches.

finishing

1. Weave in any loose ends. Then fold your square diagonally to form a triangle.

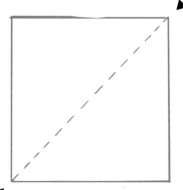

2. Sew one side of the triangle closed.
3. Pour a little bit of catnip into the triangle, put some of your stuffing on top, and then add more catnip.

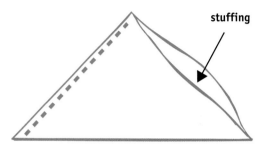

stuffing

4. Being careful to keep the catnip inside, sew the other side of the triangle closed.
5. Pull the far corners of the triangle together to form a wonton shape. Hold the corners together while you sew them, working your needle on the "inside" of the corners so your stitching won't be visible. Give to happy cat.

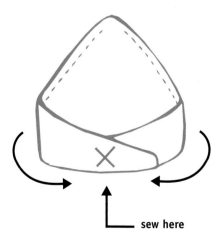

sew here

more -->

egg roll

measurements

Unfinished: 10 x 8 inches
Finished: 5½ x 1½ inches

materials

- 1 skein of Brown Sheep Lamb's Pride [100% wool; 200 yds per 113g skein] (Color used here: Sunburst Gold) [Note: You'll need about 50 yards of yarn per egg roll.]
- 1 pair size 5 (3.75mm) straight needles
- Tapestry needle
- Cotton balls, yarn scraps, and bits of fabric for stuffing
- Catnip (optional)

gauge

- 24 stitches/30 rows = 4 inches in stockinette stitch (See tip about gauge on page 48.)

pattern

- Cast on 60 stitches.
- Work in stockinette (knit 1 row, purl 1 row) until piece measures 3½ inches, ending with a purl row.
- Next row: Bind off first 12 stitches, then knit to end.
- Next row: Bind off first 12 stitches, then purl to end. You should now have 36 stitches on your needle.
- Knit 2 rows without binding off any stitches.
- Next row (decrease row): Knit 1, k2tog, knit to last 3 stitches, SSK, knit 1.
- Continue working in stockinette, repeating the above decrease row every 4 rows (you'll do it 5 more times), until there are 24 stitches left.
- Knit every row until entire piece measures 8 inches.
- Bind off all stitches.

finishing

1. Weave in any loose ends. Then place knitted piece wrong side up.
2. Place the stuffing and catnip in center of wide end. Fold the "tabs" along each side over stuffing.

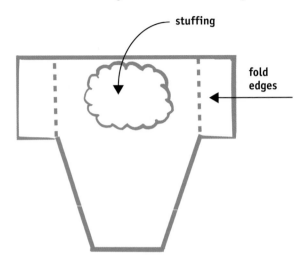

stuffing

fold edges

3. Being careful not to spill the catnip, start at the catnip end and roll the egg roll very tightly. Sew the short seam of flap to "body" of egg roll. Offer to cat in need of an appetizer!

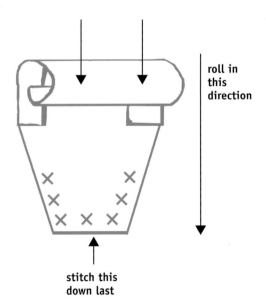

roll in this direction

stitch this down last

Meet Spike, the only family member who loves yarn more than I do!

stripey scarf

PATTERN BY SHANNON OKEY

skills casting on, knit stitch, joining new yarn, increasing (k1fb), decreasing (k2tog tbl), binding off, weaving in ends

This simple scarf looks complex because of the yarn, not the pattern. I used a Textural Yarn Kit by Erica Weiner, which includes more than 20 different types and colors of yarn in one big skein. Use any mixture of yarns and colors you like—just attach the new color whenever you want to switch (as on page 26) and keep going!

materials

- As many different colors and types of yarn as you want, totaling approximately 160–200 yards
- 1 pair size 6 (4mm) or 8 (5mm) straight needles
- Tapestry needle

gauge

This will vary depending on the types of yarn used.

pattern

- Cast on 3 stitches.
- Row 1: Knit.
- Row 2: K1fb, knit to last stitch, k1fb.
- Repeat rows 1 and 2 until you have 33 stitches.
- Next row: Knit.
- Next row (diagonal garter stitch): K1fb, knit to last 2 stitches, k2tog tbl.
- Next row: Knit.
- Alternate between 1 row diagonal garter stitch, 1 row knit, until scarf is desired length, ending with a knit row.
- Next row (decrease row): K2tog tbl, knit to last 2 stitches, k2tog tbl.
- Now alternate between 1 knit row, 1 decrease row, until you have 3 stitches left.
- Bind off these 3 stitches.

finishing

Weave in any loose ends.

finished measurements

The scarf pictured measures 5 x 56 inches, but the length and width will vary according to yarns used.

GETTING
around

5

You can use circular
needles just like straight
needles, of course,
but here you'll learn
how to use circulars the
way they're designed
to be used—to make
tube shapes!

working with circular needles

Although you may already be working on circular needles to make flat pieces, using them to make tubes is called **knitting in the round**. Hats and leg warmers knitted in the round fit better and require less shaping effort than those knitted flat. Here's how to get started.

1 Cast on the required number of stitches. Then spread them out along the entire length of the needle. Line up the bottom loops of yarn so they're all running along the "bottom" of the needle. This will keep you from twisting the round when you start to knit. Don't skip this step, because you'll have to start again from the beginning if you do.

tip

When you work with circular needles, each row is called a "round."

2 Place the needle side that's connected to the yarn ball in your right hand (or your dominant hand) and insert it into the first stitch on the left side. (Insert a stitch marker first if the pattern tells you to mark the start of the round, because that's where you are.) Now knit as usual.

When you get back to where you started, just keep going. You may notice that the first stitch—the "connector" stitch—is a little loose for the first few rounds. It should tighten up if you tug gently on the loose yarn end.

ponytail roll-brim hat

PATTERN BY SHANNON OKEY

skills casting on, knitting in the round, using stitch markers, knit stitch, increasing (make 1), decreasing (k2tog), using double-pointed needles, binding off, weaving in ends

My knitting teacher and friend Lucy Lee taught me a version of this basic pattern a few years ago. Once you can knit this plain hat, you'll be able to make hundreds of different hats just by changing the yarn or adding purl stitches for patterns. Our ponytail version is an example of a small change that makes a big difference—by binding off a small section of stitches, you can pull your ponytail through a hole in the back. Great for skiing!

materials

- Hat on right: 2 skeins of Muench Tessin [43% wool, 35% acrylic, 22% cotton; 110 yds per 100g skein] (Color used here: 824 Fuschia) / Hat on left: 1 skein of Brown Sheep Lamb's Pride [100% wool; 200 yds per 113g skein] (Color used here: Periwinkle)
- 1 16-inch size 8 (5mm) circular needle
- 1 set size 8 (5mm) double-pointed needles (optional)
- Stitch marker
- Row counter
- Tapestry needle

gauge

- Approximately 4 stitches/4–5 rows = 1 inch [Note: Most worsted weight yarns will work in this pattern. Make a swatch first or try the hat on after the first inch of knitting. It should fit without feeling too tight.]

Here's the hat without the hole (left), and with it (right).

pattern

- Cast 80 stitches onto the circular needle. Place a stitch marker at start of round. Join to knit in the round, being careful not to twist.
- Knit 1 round. Then continue knitting every round until hat measures about 3½ inches.
- Next round: Now it's time to make the hole for your ponytail (if you don't want the hole, skip this step and the next one). At the marker, bind off the next 10 stitches. Knit remainder of round.
- Next round: Knit until you reach the start of your ponytail hole, then add 10 new stitches using the make 1 method. Knit remainder of round. You should now have 80 stitches.
- Continue knitting all stitches. Keep going until your hat measures 6 inches or longer, as the first inch or so of the brim will roll up. Then start shaping the top as follows, beginning each new round at the marker.

shaping

- Round 1: *K2tog, knit 8* to end of round.
- Round 2: Knit.
- Round 3: *K2tog, knit 7* to end of round.
- Round 4: Knit.
- Round 5: *K2tog, knit 6* to end of round.
- Round 6: Knit.
- Round 7: *K2tog, knit 5* to end of round.
- Round 8: Knit.
- Round 9: *K2tog, knit 4* to end of round.
- Round 10: Knit. (You may want to switch to DPNs or knit on 2 circular needles at this point. See page 63 for more on using DPNs.)
- Round 11: *K2tog, knit 3* to end of round.
- Round 12: Knit.
- Round 13: *K2tog, knit 2* to end of round.
- Round 14: Knit.
- Round 15: *K2tog, knit 1* to end of round.
- Round 16: Knit. You should now have 16 stitches left on your needle.

finishing

Break the yarn, leaving a 12-inch tail. Thread the yarn onto a tapestry needle and slide it through the remaining stitches a few times, removing the knitting needle as you go. Pull the tail to close the circle and secure it with a double-knot. Weave in any loose ends.

tip

If you want a pointy top instead of a flat, rounded one, keep decreasing until only 2 stitches remain, then bind off.

HOW TO USE STITCH MARKERS

When knitting in the round, you usually need to keep track of where the round begins, or where you need to do something (like a decrease). This is where stitch markers come in handy. They slide onto your needle between two stitches and serve as a reminder of where the round begins. When you get to the marker, just slide it from your left needle onto your right and keep going. They're not just for circular needles, though—you can use them between stitches on any kind of needle!

heartfelt roll-brim hat

PATTERN BY SHANNON OKEY

skills casting on, knitting in the round, using stitch markers, knit stitch, purl stitch, decreasing (k2tog), using double-pointed needles, binding off, weaving in ends

H ere's the same basic hat, but with a stitch pattern worked in. Try this one, or design your own unique hat with its very own pattern!

materials

- 1 skein of Brown Sheep Lamb's Pride [100% wool; 200 yds per 113g skein] (Color used here: Blue Blood Red)
- 1 16-inch size 8 (5mm) circular needle
- 1 set size 8 (5mm) double-pointed needles (optional)
- Stitch marker
- Row counter
- Tapestry needle

pattern

- Cast 80 stitches onto circular needle. Place a stitch marker at start of round. Join to knit in the round, being careful not to twist.
- Round 1: Knit.
- Rounds 2–4: *Knit 4, purl 4* to end of round.
- Rounds 5–6: *Purl 4, knit 4* to end of round.
- Rounds 7–8: *Knit 4, purl 4* to end of round.
- Rounds 9–14: Knit.
- Rounds 15–22: Follow the chart to add a heart design, reading each row from right to left.
- Rounds 23–28: Knit.
- Rounds 29–30: Purl.

shaping and finishing

Follow the directions on page 55.

make it your own

Knitting a heart (or any other shape) on plain stockinette using purl stitches is easy—just think of stockinette stitch like graph paper. Every "square" is a stitch. Color in the shape you want on graph paper and figure out how many stitches wide it is. Divide this number into 80. This is how many times you can repeat that shape going around. When you knit the shape in purl stitches, you follow your graphed chart from the bottom up.

HEART PATTERN

																							round
	X	X	X				X	X	X				X	X	X				X	X	X		22
X	X	X	X	X		X	X	X	X	X		X	X	X	X	X		X	X	X	X	X	21
X	X	X	X	X	X	X	X	X	X	X		X	X	X	X	X	X	X	X	X	X	X	20
	X	X	X	X	X	X	X	X	X				X	X	X	X	X	X	X	X	X		19
		X	X	X	X	X	X	X						X	X	X	X	X	X	X			18
			X	X	X	X	X									X	X	X	X	X				17
				X	X	X											X	X	X					16
					X													X						15

1 square = 1 stitch

x = purl stitch; all other stitches are knit

<-- read chart from right to left

web

Want to ask a question? Just go to www.knitgrrl.com.

d.i.y. leg warmers

PATTERN BY STACEY IRVINE

skills casting on, knitting in the round, using double-pointed needles, knit stitch, purl stitch, increasing (make 1), decreasing (k2tog, SSK), binding off, weaving in ends

These leg warmers are knit in one piece from the knee to the ankle—there are no seams. Make them in a solid color or add a spiral stripe or two. When you're done, make them your own by adding beading or embroidery in whatever design you want. This pair was knitted by Stacey and embroidered by Jenny Hart.

materials

- 2 skeins of Cascade 220 [100% wool; 220 yds per 100g skein] (Color used here: Cream)
- 1 16-inch size 6 (4mm) circular needle, or size needed to obtain gauge
- 1 set size 4 (3.5mm) double-pointed needles (or 2 sizes smaller than your circular needles)
- Row counter
- Stitch markers
- Yarn and tapestry needle for embroidery (optional)

gauge

- 18 stitches/26 rows = 4 inches in stockinette stitch [Note: this is one project where row gauge really matters!]

size

PATTERN	LENGTH	CIRCUMFERENCE AT TOP	CIRCUMFERENCE AT BOTTOM
Small	12½ inches	11 inches	6½ inches
Medium	16 inches	13 inches	8 inches
Large	18 inches	15 inches	9 inches

tip

Double-pointed needles (DPNs) are used in this project to make the ribbing at the ankle, which is too small for a circular needle to handle. If you haven't knitted on DPNs yet, flip ahead to page 63 and learn how to use them before getting started.

pattern

Find your size in the chart above, then follow the directions given below for that size.

small

⊚ Using the DPNs, cast on 32 stitches. Cast your stitches onto 1 DPN, then spread the stitches evenly across 2 more. Place a stitch marker at start of round. Join, being careful not to twist the work.

⊚ Rounds 1–13 (ribbing): *Knit 1, purl 1* to end of round.

⊚ Slip all stitches from the DPNs to the larger circular needle, as if you were moving them to a stitch holder.

⊚ Round 14 (increase round): *Knit 5, make 1* until last 2 stitches, then knit 2. You should have 38 stitches.

⊚ Rounds 15–29: Knit.

⊚ Round 30 (decrease round): K2tog, knit to last 2 stitches, SSK. You should now have 36 stitches.

⊚ Continue in stockinette stitch, repeating decrease round every 15 rounds (4 more times). After round 90, you should have only 28 stitches.

⊚ Rounds 91–96: Knit.

⊚ Slip stitches back to 3 smaller DPNs, divided evenly.

⊚ Round 97: *K2tog, knit 5* to end of round. You should now have 24 stitches.

⊚ Rounds 98–111 (ribbing): *Knit 1, purl 1* to end of round.

⊚ Bind off loosely.

medium

⊚ Using the DPNs, cast on 40 stitches. Cast your stitches onto 1 DPN, then spread the stitches evenly across 2 more. Place a stitch marker at start of round. Join, being careful not to twist the work.

⊚ Rounds 1–13 (ribbing): *Knit 1, purl 1* to end of round.

⊚ Slip all stitches from the DPNs to the larger circular needle, as if you were moving them to a stitch holder.

⊚ Round 14 (increase round): *Knit 3, make 1* to last 4 stitches, then knit 4. You should have 52 stitches.

⊚ Rounds 15–21: Knit.

⊚ Round 22 (decrease round): K2tog, knit to last 2 stitches, SSK. You should now have 50 stitches.

⊚ Continue in stockinette stitch, repeating decrease round every 11 rows (7 more times). After round 99, you should have only 36 stitches.

⊚ Rounds 100–103: Knit.

⊚ Slip stitches back to 3 smaller DPNs, divided evenly.

⊚ Round 104: *Knit 4, k2tog* to end of round. You should now have 30 stitches.

⊚ Rounds 105–117 (ribbing): *Knit 1, purl 1* to end of round.

⊚ Bind off loosely.

large

- Using the DPNs, cast on 50 stitches. Cast your stitches onto 1 DPN, then spread the stitches evenly across 2 more. Place a stitch marker at start of round. Join, being careful not to twist the work.
- Rounds 1–13 (ribbing): *Knit 1, purl 1* to end of round.
- Slip all stitches from the DPNs to the larger circular needle, as if you were moving them to a stitch holder.
- Round 14 (increase round): *Knit 3, make 1* to last 2 stitches, then knit 2. You should have 66 stitches.
- Rounds 15–22: Knit.
- Round 23 (decrease round): K2tog, knit to last 2 stitches, SSK. You should now have 64 stitches.
- Continue in stockinette stitch, repeating decrease round every 9 rows (12 more times). After round 131, you should have only 40 stitches.
- Slip stitches back to 3 smaller DPNs, divided evenly.
- Round 132: *Knit 3, k2tog* to end of round. You should now have 32 stitches.
- Row 133–145 (ribbing): *Knit 1, purl 1* to end of round.
- Bind off loosely.

finishing

Weave in any loose ends. See page 86 for tips on adding your own embroidered decoration.

web

Want to meet the designers? Go to www.knitgrrl.com.

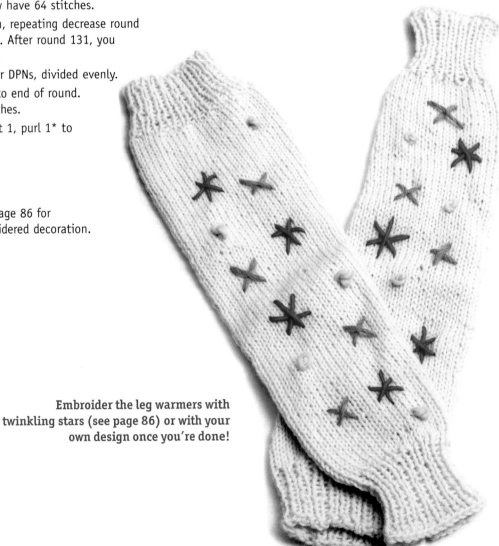

Embroider the leg warmers with twinkling stars (see page 86) or with your own design once you're done!

make your own stitch markers

Stitch markers are used to keep track of where you are in your knitting, plain and simple. But they don't have to be plain! Why use little scraps of yarn to mark your place (useful in a pinch, but not very glamorous) when you can have beautiful, personalized markers? Most markers come in sets of five, with one that's different from the others. Make yours however you like!

For markers that will hold up over time, buy clear plastic fishing line. You can find it in hardware stores, or the jewelry-making section of craft stores. Embroidery floss is colorful and works well if you don't have fishing line.

Cut a 5-inch length of fishing line or embroidery floss, and string on the small beads for about 1 inch. Finish with a larger, decorative bead if desired—I used a starfish. Tie the line or floss tightly, knot three times, and trim the ends off. Voilà! You have a gorgeous, one-of-a-kind stitch marker.

FOR EACH MARKER YOU WILL NEED:

- ◉ Clear plastic fishing line (embroidery floss will also work)
- ◉ Assorted small beads
- ◉ 1 decorative bead (not too heavy!)

SEEING DOUBLE

6

Double the fun by adding more colors and a new type of needle! This chapter will show you how to knit with more than one color at the same time. You'll also learn about double-pointed needles, or DPNs, which are used to knit smaller tubes than a circular needle can handle.

how to use double-pointed needles

When you knit on DPNs, each row is called a "round," just as with circular needles. To use them, cast the number of required stitches onto one of the needles (they usually come in sets of four or five). Then divide the stitches evenly among three or four needles by slipping the stitches, one at a time, onto the other needles, as if you were transferring them to a stitch holder.

Always leave one needle empty as your "working" needle. As you knit from a "full" needle onto the working needle, the full needle will empty and become your new working needle. The strangest thing about using DPNs is how the other needles "dangle" when you're not using them. To keep stitches from sliding off the dangling needles, just center them in the middle of the needles.

1 Cast all of the stitches onto the first needle.

2 Divide the stitches evenly among three needles by slipping them from the first needle onto the other two.

3 Until the round has been joined, the needles will hang loose in your hands, but that's okay.

4 Hold the "working" (empty) needle in your dominant hand and knit from the start of the round. When you've knit all the stitches on the first DPN, it becomes your new working needle.

5 Knit all the way around. Each time you finish the stitches on a DPN, that becomes your new working needle. Be careful not to twist the stitches.

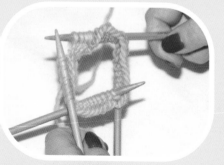

6 After knitting a few rows, you'll see a small tube begin to take shape.

knitting with more than one color

Since color is so much fun to work with, you should know how to use multiple colors in your work. The Stripey Scarf (page 51) showed you how switching yarns as you go can create a colorful scarf.

But what if you want to use more than one color in the same row? There are different techniques you can use. The two most common are **intarsia** (also called "picture knitting") and **Fair Isle**. Many, many books have been written on color knitting styles. Many arguments have taken place about the "right" way to do color knitting. For the record: What works for you is what's best.

In this chapter, the Text-Messaging Mittens pattern uses multiple colors in the same row, and the method described involves holding both yarn

web

Want to post a photo of your finished project? Do it at www.knitgrrl.com.

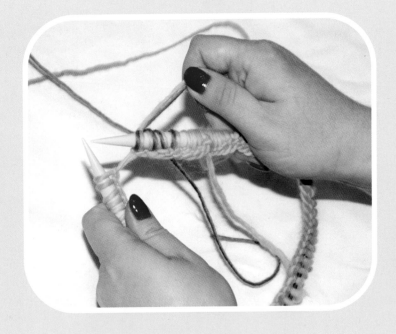

To knit with two colors in the same row, just hold strands of both and use each color when you want to. Let the color you're not using dangle in the back until you want to use it again.

colors in your hand at once. When you want to knit a stitch with Color 1, use that yarn and let the other yarn dangle on the wrong side without knitting it (called **carrying the yarn**). When you want to knit a stitch with Color 2, switch to that yarn and carry Color 1. It's easy! The only thing you need to watch out for when you carry the other yarn behind the work (which is called a **yarn float**, or just **float**) is that you don't pull the float too tightly. If you do, it will cause a pucker on the public side of the work.

Many modern scarf patterns use fancy novelty yarns together with plain wool yarns to create a particular effect. In almost all of these patterns, the fancy yarn is carried with the plain yarn and knitted simultaneously. You can do this with colors, too. Try knitting with two strands of different colored yarn for a few inches, then knitting with just Color 1, then with Color 2, and back to both at once. The possibilities are endless!

PATTERN BY STEFANIE JAPEL

skills casting on, knit stitch, purl stitch, joining new yarn, increasing (make 1), decreasing (k2tog), weaving in ends, seaming, I-cord

These musical device cozies will keep your cassette/CD player or iPod safe and warm—and with the matching covers, your headphones will be as stylish as your music. This pattern does not use much yarn. If you want to make a solid-color or two-color cover instead, you will only need about two skeins of yarn.

measurements

Unfinished music player cozy: about 10 x 6 inches
Unfinished headphone covers: about 4 x 5 inches each

materials

- 5 colors of Brown Sheep Cotton Fleece [80% cotton, 20% wool; 215 yds per 3.5oz skein] (I used leftover scraps of yarn; you can use whatever colors you have on hand.)
- 1 pair size 4 (3.5mm) straight needles
- Row counter
- Tapestry needle

gauge

16 stitches/24 rows = 4 inches

tip

To keep track of which color is which, cut a small piece of each yarn color and tape it to a piece of paper. Label them Color 1, Color 2, Color 3, and so on. You can then refer to the sheet instead of trying to keep five different color names and numbers straight!

music player cozy

- Using Color 1, cast on 32 stitches.
- Work in garter stitch (knit all rows) for 5 rows.
- Switch to stockinette stitch (knit 1 row, purl 1 row). Work 7 rows in Color 1.
- Using Color 3, work 2 rows.
- Using Color 1, work 2 rows.
- Using Color 4, work 7 rows.
- Using Color 2, work 2 rows.
- Using Color 5, work 1 row.
- Using Color 3, work 9 rows.
- Using Color 1, work 1 row.
- Using Color 4, work 2 rows.
- Using Color 5, work 7 rows.
- Using Color 2, work 1 row.
- Using Color 3, work 2 rows.
- Using Color 1, work 7 rows.
- Using Color 5, work 4 rows.
- Using Color 4, work 4 rows.
- Staying with Color 4, work 5 rows in garter stitch, then bind off.

Ties (make 2)

Using Color 2, cast on 3 stitches. Work in I-cord for 5 inches. Bind off. (See page 84 for more on making I-cord.)

finishing

1. Weave in loose ends. Fold knitted piece in half lengthwise. Sew up each side seam with a tapestry needle.

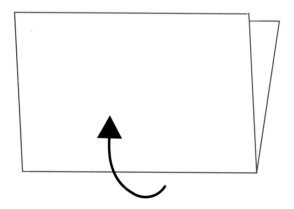

2. Sew one tie inside the center of each side (front and back). Insert music player!

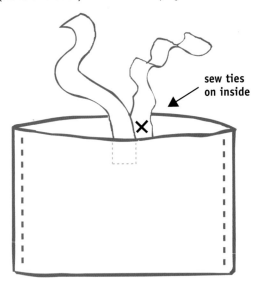

sew ties on inside

belt loop (optional)

- With Color 2, cast on 20 stitches.
- Work in garter stitch (knit every row) for 5 rows.
- Row 6: Knit.
- Row 7: Knit 5, purl to last 5 stitches, knit 5.
- Repeat rows 6 and 7. Do this 5 times, for 10 more rows.
- Work in garter stitch for 5 rows. Bind off.
- Sew the rectangle to the back of the cozy, like this:

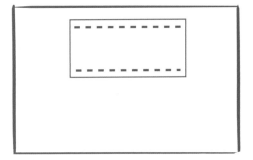

headphone covers (make 2)

- Using Color 5, cast on 13 stitches.
- Rows 1–6: Start each row with an increase (make 1), then work remainder of row in stockinette (knit 1 row, purl 1 row).
- Rows 7–9: Switch to Color 1. Start each row with an increase (make 1), then work remainder of row in stockinette.
- Rows 10–14: Switch to Color 2. Work rows even in stockinette, with no increase.
- Rows 15–16: Switch to Color 4 and work even.
- Rows 17–19: Switch to Color 1 and work even.
- Rows 20–23: Start each row with a decrease (k2tog), then work remainder of row in stockinette.
- Rows 24–28: Switch to Color 3 and continue decreasing as above. You should end up with 13 stitches.
- Bind off.

finishing

Weave in loose ends. To attach the covers to your headphones, use yarn the color of the outside stripe and sew around the edge onto your headphones on either side. If you don't want to attach them permanently, sew a piece of yarn around the edge of each cover with a long, loose stitch. Place them around the headphones and pull tight, like a drawstring. Secure with a knot.

Attach a cover to each headphone for a unique way to tune in!

soda cozy

PATTERN BY STEFANIE JAPEL

skills casting on, using double-pointed needles, knit stitch, purl stitch, using stitch markers, binding off, weaving in ends

Keep cold things cold and hot things hot while insulating your hands from either extreme! These fun and fluffy cozies are at home on both soda cans and cups of hot cocoa. They're a great gift if you need to whip something up in a hurry, too.

finished measurements
About 5 inches tall

materials
- MC: 1 skein of Lana Grossa Dito [60% cotton, 40% acrylic; 135m per 50g skein] (Colors used here: light blue 04 and dark blue 016)
- CC: 1 skein of Lana Grossa Basics Venezia Color [100% polyester; 90m per 50g skein] (Colors used here: 012 and 405)
- 1 set size 3 (3.25mm) double-pointed needles
- 1 set size 5 (3.75mm) double-pointed needles (or size needed to obtain gauge)
- Row counter
- Stitch markers
- Tapestry needle

gauge
22 stitches/28 rows = 4 inches using MC

20 stitches/24 rows = 4 inches using both yarns together on larger needles

pattern
- Using smaller DPNs and MC, cast on 36 stitches. Divide evenly over 3 needles. Place a stitch marker at start of round. Join to knit in the round, being careful not to twist.
- Rounds 1–7 (ribbing): *Knit 1, purl 1* to end of round.
- Rounds 8–17: Switch to larger needles. Holding both yarns together, work in garter stitch (knit every round).
- Rounds 18–23: Drop fur yarn and work in stockinette stitch (knit 1 round, purl 1 round) with MC only.
- Rounds 24–33: Work in garter stitch holding both yarns.
- Bind off loosely.

finishing
Weave in any yarn ends.

tip

Turn this into a cozy for your mobile phone by sewing the bottom shut!

text-messaging mittens

PATTERN BY HEATHER BRACK

skills casting on, using double-pointed needles, using stitch markers, knit stitch, purl stitch, joining new yarn, increasing (make 1), decreasing (k2tog), using a stitch holder, picking up stitches, binding off, weaving in ends

Have you ever noticed how hard it is to text-message when you're wearing mittens? Just flip off the thumbs of these cool mittens and you'll be able to press tiny phone buttons, change the volume on your iPod, or just scratch your nose—all while keeping your hands nice and warm. The mittens have a two-color pattern for extra pizzazz, but you can knit them all in one color if you prefer.

materials

- 2 skeins of Cascade 220 in different colors [100% wool; 220 yds per 100g skein] (Colors used here: [MC] 8339 and [CC] 4002)
- 1 set (you'll need 5) size 7 (4.5mm) double-pointed needles (or size needed to obtain gauge)
- Row counter
- Stitch markers
- Stitch holder
- Tapestry needle

gauge

20 stitches/24 rows = 4 inches in stockinette stitch

pattern

- Using MC, cast on 40 stitches.
- Divide evenly on 4 DPNs. Place stitch marker at start of round. Join without twisting to knit in the round.
- Knit 1 round.
- Attach CC and knit 4 rounds.
- Zigzag stripe: Work the next 4 rounds as follows. You can hold both yarns in one hand, or one in the left and one in the right—whichever is more comfortable.
  Round 1: *Knit 1 with CC, knit 1 with MC* to end of round.
  Round 2: Knit all stitches with MC.
  Round 3: *Knit 1 with MC, knit 1 with CC* to end of round.
  Round 4: Knit all stitches with CC.

- Repeat the zigzag stripe pattern 3 more times (for 12 more rounds). If you are not comfortable knitting with 2 colors at the same time, knit regular stripes instead by alternating 2 rounds in each color for 16 rounds.
- Knit 2 rounds with MC. In the second round, place stitch markers to prepare to knit the thumb gusset. Place the first marker 2 stitches from the end of the second needle. Place the other marker 2 stitches into the third needle. There should be 4 stitches between the markers.

Thumb Gusset (for left mitten)

- Round 1: Continue with MC. Knit to first marker, slip marker to right needle, make 1, knit to end of round.
- Round 2: Knit.
- Repeat rounds 1 and 2 until there are 9 stitches between the markers.
  [Note: This is the only part of the pattern that changes for the right mitten. See instructions at end of pattern.]

Palm

- Keep using MC. Knit to first marker, slip the stitches between the markers onto a stitch holder, knit to end of round.
- Next round: Knit to stitch holder, then add 4 new stitches using the make 1 method. Continue knitting to end of round.
- Knit all rounds even until the palm reaches the top of your pinkie finger.
- Work rounds 3 and 4 of the zigzag stripe pattern (or knit 2 rounds of CC).
- Switch to MC and knit 2 rounds.

Shape the Top

- Keep using MC. *Knit 3, k2tog* to end of round. You should now have 32 stitches.
- Knit 1 round.
- *Knit 2, k2tog* to end of round. You should have 24 stitches.
- Knit 1 round.
- *Knit 1, k2tog* to end of round. You should have 16 stitches remaining.
- Knit 1 round.
- *K2tog* all the way around for 1 round.
- Break yarn and thread through remaining 8 stitches twice. Pull tight and secure end.

Knit the Thumb

- Divide the stitches on the stitch holder between 2 DPNs.
- Using CC and a third DPN, pick up 6 stitches across the top of the thumbhole (see page 76 to learn how).
- Knit to the last stitch in the round.
- Slip the last stitch onto the first needle. K2tog, knit to the last stitch on the needle. Slip the last stitch to the second needle and k2tog, then knit to end of round.
- Knit all rounds even until the thumb reaches your knuckle when you try it on.
- Bind off 7 stitches on the inside of the thumb (the side facing your palm), knit to end of round.
- At the start of the next round, add 7 new stitches using the make 1 method, then knit to end of round.
- Knit all rounds until it covers your thumb.
- Knit 1, then *k2tog* to end of round.
- Break yarn and thread twice through the remaining 7 stitches. Pull tight and secure tail.

This pattern will give you a left mitten. To make the right mitten, do everything the same except for the thumb gusset, which you should knit as follows:

- Round 1: Continue with MC. Knit until 1 stitch before second marker, make 1, slip marker to right needle, knit to end of round.
- Round 2: Knit.
- Repeat rounds 1 and 2 until there are 9 stitches between the markers.

Call your friends. Tune your iPod. Text your mother. Do it all with these awesome mittens!

more color!

There are many ways to knit with more than one color of yarn, including Fair Isle and intarsia-style patterning mentioned earlier. Our mittens use two colors to create a zigzag stripe. At first it may seem hard to knit with two colors at the same time (and you can opt out of doing it if you want). Try practicing with a test swatch before tackling the zigzag stripe—once you're comfortable knitting with two different color yarns, it will be that much easier to do the pattern. And if you really like using more than one color at once, go for it! Why not three or four colors? You're the designer!

make your own knitter's hand salve

All that knitting can make your hands rough! And when your hands and nails are rough, they will no doubt catch on your yarn. (Carrying a nail file in your knitting bag is a good idea for this reason alone—plus you can use it to sand down rough needle tips if you need to.) Give your hands a treat with this recipe for knitter's hand salve. It also makes a great gift for knitting pals.

Pour the salt into a mixing bowl. Add the honey and olive oil. Mix together with a fork until thoroughly combined. Add essential oils if you like (but not too much!), and scoop into your jar. This can be stored in the fridge for up to two weeks. If you're in a hurry, you can also mix it on the go in your hand! Just keep the amounts of each ingredient except the essential oils roughly equal.

To use, take a spoonful of the mixture and rub it in your palms until it's evenly spread out. Rub all over the backs of your hands and rinse away with warm water. Your skin will stay smooth for a long time!

YOU WILL NEED:

- 1/4 cup kosher salt
- 1/4 cup honey
- 1/4 cup olive oil
- Mixing bowl
- Fork
- A few drops of essential oils, like lavender or orange (optional)
- Small, clean jar (jelly jars with screw-top lids are good)

I FELT IT WAS TIME

7

We're all expert *accidental* felters. Wash a sweater in hot water and you end up with one that barely fits a Blythe doll. You swore you'd never do it again, but read on....

felting

Felting is the process of turning wool or other animal fibers into a more solid, dense fabric. This isn't like the sheets of craft felt you see at the sewing store—it's thicker, and can have a beautiful texture, depending on how you knit and felt it.

Felting will *not* work on plant fiber yarns like cotton, or synthetic yarns made of acrylic or polyester. Felting works because sheep's wool, llama, alpaca, and other animal fibers are a lot like human hair. When you wash your hair in hot water, you open up each fiber strand a little bit. Conditioner "glues" the hair back together again, making it shiny and smooth.

With felting, you intentionally open up the wool fiber with heat, just like washing your hair. But instead of gluing the fiber back together nicely with conditioner, you use cold water to force the wool into suddenly closing back down again. Imagine you ran out of hot water in the shower and suddenly got sprayed with cold. You'd be a little shocked, right? The wool is, too. In all the excitement, its fibers become twisted and lock together. They shrink in the process because all the airspace between the stitches is now gone. And voilà! Your piece of knitted fabric is suddenly much smaller.

Is it as simple as just throwing something knitted into a washing machine set to hot wash/cold rinse? Almost. Here are a few tips that will help you along the way:

◉ To minimize damage to your washer, periodically skim out any loose fibers. Or, you can place the object you're felting inside a pillowcase or zippered lingerie bag to contain the fibers.

◉ Use a few squirts of dishwashing detergent in the washer when you felt. For some reason, Dawn seems to work better than almost any other.

◉ If you are felting something that contains some synthetic yarn (for example, the flap of the Downtown Messenger Bag on page 78), it will usually take a little longer to felt completely.

◉ If you are trying to make something felt very solidly, throw a few pairs of jeans into the washer with it—they will help the piece to felt. The projects in this chapter illustrate the two felting extremes, the lightly-felted Lacy Double-Diamond Scarf and the hard-felted Downtown Messenger Bag. Generally, the more use or weight the object will endure, the more solidly you should felt it.

web

Need more help? Just go to www.knitgrrl.com.

IT'S a PICK-UP!

Some patterns ask you to pick up stitches at the bottom edge of already-knit stitches.
Here's how to do it.

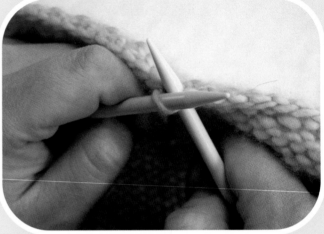

1 Insert the left-hand needle into a stitch on one edge of your knitting (the pattern will tell you which edge).

2 Insert the right-hand needle behind it, as if it were a stitch already on the needle.

3 Knit the stitch as if you were joining new yarn (see page 26).

4 Slide the completed stitch off the left needle.

Repeat steps 1–4 with the next stitch to the left. Keep picking up stitches, working from right to left, until you have the number indicated in the pattern.

blocking

Blocking is another way of saying "arranging damp knitted things to dry so they'll retain their shape, and/or stretching them a bit so you can make that inch-too-short sweater sleeve fit better," more or less. Whew! It's much easier to say "blocking," don't you agree?

Any time you wash something that was knitted, it can get pushed out of alignment. Blocking helps you put it back the way it was. Or, if it wasn't right to begin with, blocking can help you shape it more to your liking.

You may have seen someone drape a wet sweater over the washing machine lid to dry. Don't do this, unless you like having oddly shaped sweaters or want really, *really* long sleeves (the weight of the water will pull the sleeves out as they dry).

To block something correctly, remove all excess water first. (In the case of felted bags, the inside may still be damp when the outside is dry—you can stuff it gently with dry towels to absorb the moisture.) Rolling the items in a dry towel and squeezing gently is also good.

If the object is already the right size and shape, it's a question of arranging it on a towel or sweater rack (even your bed!) and leaving it until it's dry. If you want a little stretch, say for extra length in the sleeves, gently pull on them and pin them down in their new position. This is where drying items on your bed or a thick comforter really comes in handy—there's lots of space to stretch it out. "Gently pull" does not mean tug. If you tug, the knitting fairies will tangle all your yarn while you sleep. Okay, okay, I made up that last part. But if you're going to spend time making these beautiful knits, they deserve a little respect during washing and blocking.

web

Any questions about blocking? Ask them at www.knitgrrl.com.

Sometimes wool yarn will "relax" during its first bath. The hat you made suddenly doubled in size…and you'll be walking around with hat all over your face if you don't fix it. No worries: blocking to the rescue! Gently squeeze out the extra water and arrange it on your towel in the size you want it to be. For hats, stuff a dry washcloth or two inside to soak up water. Pin to the towel and wait. (In truly extreme cases, you may want to try some very light felting: Turn the item inside out and rinse it with hot water, then cold. Don't do this unless the object is much too big, otherwise you risk shrinking it too much.)

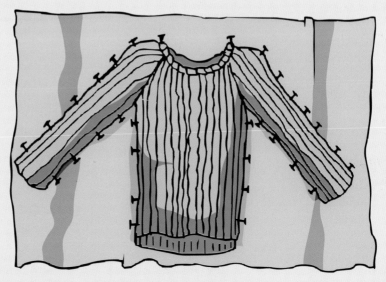

downtown messenger bag

PATTERN BY HEATHER BRACK

skills casting on, knitting in the round, using stitch markers, knit stitch, purl stitch, picking up stitches, joining new yarn, binding off, felting

This bag is the perfect size for carrying notebooks, magazines, your knitting, or just about anything else. The flap incorporates shiny multicolor yarn that, when felted with regular wool, looks like tweed fabric. Experiment with different novelty yarns in the flap! Knit a small swatch first and throw it in the washing machine to see if you like what comes out. The bag is knitted in one piece with no seams. You start with the bottom, then pick up stitches for the sides and knit the body of the bag in the round. Then you bind off stitches and knit the flap.

finished measurements

Bag after felting is 13 inches wide x 10 inches tall.

materials

- Color 1: 4 skeins of Cascade 220 [100% wool; 220 yds per 100g skein] (Color used here: 8895 Christmas Red)
- Color 2: 1 skein of Cascade 220 [100% wool; 220 yds per 100g skein] (Color used here: 8555 Black) [Note: The black yarn will need to be split into 2 equal balls so you can knit it with yarn held double.]
- Color 3: 2 balls of Cascade Malizia [60% viscose, 40% polyester; 51 yds per 50g ball] (Color used here: 5)
- 1 24–30 inch size 13 (9mm) circular needle
- 4 large stitch markers
- 2 yards of 2-inch-wide black nylon or polyester belting
- Row counter
- Stitch holder

gauge

2–3 stitches/4 rows = 1 inch before felting
[Note: Exact gauge is not critical for this project.]

pattern

- Cast on 45 stitches with Color 1 held double.
- To make the bottom of the bag, work in garter stitch (knit all rows) for 26 rows.
- Keeping all 45 stitches on the needle, slide the work across the circular needle, then place a stitch marker at the edge away from the working yarn.
- Pick up 12 stitches along what will be the short edge of the bag and place a marker. Now pick up 45 stitches along what will be the long edge and place another marker. Finally, pick up 12 stitches on what will be the other short edge. You should now have 114 stitches.
- Knit back across the row you just completed, then join to start working in the round. Place stitch marker at start of round. Knit all rounds until the piece measures about 23 inches long.
- At this point, the tube should be about 18 inches wide and 23 inches tall. These measurements are approximate, and will shrink significantly during felting.
- Knit 45 stitches. You should now be at the beginning of a short side.
- Bind off 69 stitches. You should have 45 stitches left.
- To begin the flap, knit 1 round. Break the MC, leaving a 3-inch tail.
- Join Color 2, held double, and purl 1 row.
- Join Color 3 (you are now working with 3 strands held together—2 of Color 2 and 1 of Color 3) and knit 1 row.
- Continue to work in reverse stockinette stitch (with the purl side on the outside of the bag) until flap measures about 18 inches or until you run out of yarn.
- Bind off 45 stitches.
- Trim any loose ends, but do not weave them in.

felting

To prevent the cast-off edge from deforming during felting, you may wish to sew it closed loosely with a piece of cotton or other non-felting scrap yarn. The flap can be folded back on itself and the edges lashed together.

Felt the bag in a washing machine set to hot wash/cold rinse. A small amount of detergent or dish soap may speed the process. Depending on the machine, the water temperature, the yarn, and personal preference, it may take 10–40 minutes for the fabric to felt. Check it every 5 minutes, especially if you're unfamiliar with the process. Pull it out of the machine and squeeze out the water to

really see the fabric. The flap will take longer to felt than the body of the bag. To minimize damage to the washer, periodically skim out loose fibers. You can also felt the bag inside a pillowcase or lingerie bag to contain fibers.

finishing

Stretch the bag over a sturdy box about the same size as the finished bag. If you can't find an appropriate box, you can also stretch it over the back of a chair or stuff it with rolled towels. Leave the bag stretched over the form until the outside feels dry; it may still be slightly damp inside. Depending on the weather and overall humidity, it may take a day or two. If you live in a very dry climate, it make take less than a day!

After the bag has dried completely, trim any loose yarn ends. Then attach the strap. First, prep the strap by "hemming" one end to keep it from fraying. Then use black yarn and a sharp tapestry needle to sew that end to the inside of the bag, about 3 inches below the top. To make it extra sturdy, sew in a rectangle just inside the edge of the belting, then sew an "X" through the rectangle. Adjust the length of the strap to however long you want, then hem the other end and sew that down, too.

If you'd like to add buttons and buttonholes to hold the flap closed, or trim the flap to a better size, you can cut it just as you would any other felt or fleece fabric. The fibers should remain felted together and not fray.

tip

Felting shrinks a knitted item anywhere from 10 to 25 percent. Be sure to keep this in mind if you decide to felt other things you've knitted.

lacy double-diamond scarf

PATTERN BY JILLIAN MORENO FOR ACME KNITTING COMPANY

skills casting on, knit stitch, purl stitch, double yarn over, increasing (k1fb), decreasing (SSK), picking up stitches, binding off, weaving in ends, felting

This pattern introduces the basics of knitting lace. All lace patterns are made by creating "holes" in otherwise ordinary knitted fabric with stitches called **yarn overs.** Once you master the yarn over, you'll be able to do almost any lace pattern!

finished measurements

The scarf pictured measures about 5 x 56 inches, but the length and width may vary.

materials

- MC: 2 skeins of Cascade 220 [100% wool; 220 yds per 100g skein] (Color used here: 2409 Lime)
- CC (for border): 1 skein of Cascade 220 [100% wool; 220 yds per 100g skein] (Color used here: 7804 Pink)
- 1 pair size 13 (9mm) straight needles
- Row counter
- Tapestry needle

gauge

Before felting: 10 stitches/14 rows = 4 inches in stockinette stitch

After one time through the washing machine: 14 stitches/20 rows = 4 inches

[Note: Matching the gauge exactly is not critical for this project.]

pattern

[Note: Yarn is held double throughout. Use both skeins of green yarn at the same time, but divide the pink skein into 2 equal balls when you need to knit with pink.]

- Cast on 16 stitches with MC held double. Work diamond eyelet pattern (opposite) until scarf measures 80 inches.
- Bind off loosely.

diamond eyelet pattern

- Row 1 and all following odd rows: Purl. (When purling into a double yarn over, purl the first wrap, then let the second wrap drop.)
- Row 2: Knit.
- Row 4: Knit 3, *double yarn over, SSK, knit 6* to last 3 stitches, then knit 3.
- Row 6: Knit 1, *k2tog, double yarn over, knit 1, double yarn over, SSK, knit 3* to last 2 stitches, then knit 2.
- Row 8: Knit 3, *double yarn over, SSK, knit 6* to last 3 stitches, then knit 3.
- Row 10: Knit.
- Row 12: Knit 7, *double yarn over, SSK, knit 6* to last stitch, then knit 1.
- Row 14: Knit 5, *k2tog, double yarn over, knit 1, double yarn over, SSK, knit 3* to last 3 stitches, then knit 3.
- Row 16: Knit 7, *double yarn over, SSK, knit 6* to last stitch, then knit 1.

ruffles

- With MC held double, pick up 16 stitches at one end of scarf.
- Work in stockinette stitch (purl 1 row, knit 1 row) for 3 rows, ending with a purl row.
- K1fb across all stitches. You should now have 32 stitches.
- Work in stockinette stitch for 3 rows, starting with a purl row.
- Switch to CC held double.
- K1fb across all stitches. You should have 64 stitches.
- Work 3 rows of stockinette stitch, starting with a purl row.
- Bind off loosely.
- Repeat on opposite end of scarf.

felting

Weave in loose ends. Felt the scarf gently by running it through the washing machine one time on hot wash/cold rinse (see page 75). Check your scarf every 5 minutes during the felting process and stop if it seems to be felted enough.

YO! HERE'S HOW TO DO a yarn over

A **yarn over** (or **YO**) creates a decorative hole (or eyelet) in the knitted fabric. To do a yarn over, just bring the yarn to the front between stitches by drawing it through the space between the two needles. Wrap the yarn around ("over") the top of the right needle and bring it back to where it was. Then just do a normal knit stitch. The extra wrap will disappear when you knit the next row, forming a hole.

To do a **double yarn over** (or **YO2**), as used in the Lacy Double-Diamond Scarf pattern, do the same thing but wrap the yarn *twice* around the needle. Then do a normal knit stitch. When you come to this stitch in the next row, let both extra wraps of yarn drop. This creates an elongated, decorative stitch.

To do a yarn over, wrap the yarn once around the right needle before doing a knit stitch.

To do a double yarn over, wrap the yarn twice around the needle before doing a knit stitch.

makin' IT FANCY

8

Here's how to add that extra bit of decoration—from pom-poms on the top of a hat to cables on the bottom of a scarf, and everything in between!

pom-poms

Pom-poms are fun to put on the top of a hat or at the ends of a scarf. They're easy to make, too. Here's how.

1 Wrap yarn around a folded-over piece of cardboard. The more yarn you wrap, the fluffier your pom-pom will be. Thread a tapestry needle with the same yarn. Pass the needle through the cardboard and pull through on the end with the open fold.

2 Tie the piece of yarn tightly on top, over the wrapped yarn.

3 Use scissors to cut through the yarn on the other side.

4 Tighten the knot and secure it with a double knot. Then fluff!

tip

To make a multi-colored pom-pom, hold several strands of different-colored yarn together as you wrap them around the cardboard. Use any color yarn to tie the strands together.

i-cord

I-cord is great for trimming the edges of hats, scarves, purses, and just about anything else. It's also fun to wind all over a hat or scarf and then sew down with the same yarn threaded through a tapestry needle. Felted I-cord is one of the easiest kinds of purse handles there is to make—just throw it in the washer and it's ready to go. (Don't forget to make it longer than you need, to account for shrinkage.) Here's how to make it.

pattern

- Cast on 3–5 stitches, depending on how thick you want the cord. You can use a circular needle or 2 double-pointed needles.
- Knit the first row.
- Slide the knitting to the other end of the needle.
- Pull the thread tight across the back of the stitches as you knit the next row (see photo below).
- Slide the knitting across again, and continue to knit as above.
- After knitting back and forth a few rows, tug on the bottom of the knitted tube that is developing. You'll see it even out and turn into a nice, smooth cord.

To knit I-cord, slide each row of stitches to the other side of the needle and pull the yarn tight across the back as you knit the next row.

cables

Cables are another way to dress up the plainest of knitting patterns. They can be very simple, or very complex. For this reason, cable patterns are usually presented in a chart.

Cables are made by rearranging the order of stitches on your needle—think of it as twisting them, like a pretzel. When you reach a **cable crossing** in the pattern chart, you just slip the next few stitches

(your pattern will tell you how many) to a spare needle. (There are special **cable needles** for this, but a double-pointed needle works just as well!) You then hold that needle either in front or in back of your knitting (again, the pattern will tell you) while you knit the next few stitches on your main needle. To finish the crossing, you knit the "held" stitches off the cable needle, and then continue along the row.

1 Slip a few stitches (your pattern will tell you how many) to a spare needle.

2 Hold the stitches in back of your knitting (shown on the left) or in front (shown on the right), according to the pattern directions.

3 Knit the next few stitches on your main needle.

4 Now knit the stitches from the spare needle.

5 Continue knitting the rest of the row.

embroidery

Most embroidery done on knitted items is made using something called the **duplicate stitch**. True to its name, this stitch is done by using a tapestry needle to go over (or "duplicate") the "v" of your knitted stitches with a different colored yarn. But you're not limited to duplicate stitch! Here are two other stitches you can use: the straight stitch and the French knot. These were used on the D.I.Y. Leg Warmers (page 58) and can be used to spark up any knitted item. Use these stitches—or others you may know how to do—to create your own designs.

The D.I.Y. Leg Warmers (page 58) were embroidered with blue French knots (which form little bumps) and red and yellow stars made with a straight stitch.

STRAIGHT STITCH

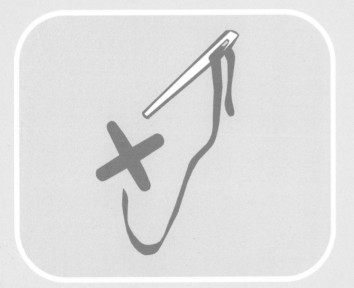

The straight stitch looks like a long sewing stitch, and can be made as long or short as you like. To form a star, just make three stitches that cross in the center.

FRENCH KNOT

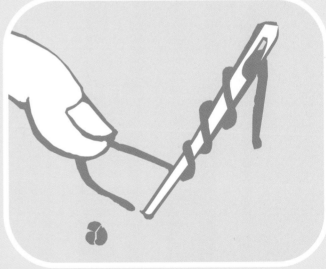

To make a French knot, push the needle through from the back side of your fabric where you want the knot to be. Wrap the yarn around the needle tip three times, then push it back down through your knitted fabric near where it came out.

embroidery by jenny hart

In some corners of the crafty universe, Jenny Hart needs no introduction, but just in case you've been floating around in a galaxy far, far away, here goes! Jenny's known for making embroidery cool—her company, Sublime Stitching, sells iron-on patterns that you can stitch on cloth. But, just for you, she's designed some simple patterns you can use with a tapestry needle and yarn on knitted fabric.

The easiest way to transfer these patterns onto your knitted object (or any other pattern you might draw for yourself) is to photocopy them onto plain white paper. Cut out the pattern you want, with a little extra around its edges, and pin it to the place you want to embroider using safety pins. Now choose a stitch to use, load up your tapestry needle with yarn, and stitch along the outline of the design. At the beginning, leave a tail of yarn on the wrong side to weave into the knitted fabric. When you're done, carefully tear off the paper pattern, leaving only your embroidered design.

nakiska alpine headband

PATTERN BY AMY SWENSON

skills casting on, knitting in the round, using stitch markers, knit stitch, purl stitch, increasing (make 1), decreasing (k2tog), making cables, binding off, weaving in ends

This headband, named for a ski resort in Calgary, is comfy, warm, and looks much fancier than it is to knit. You'll want to make one in wool to wear when shoveling the driveway and another in cotton to wear year round. In this pattern, instructions are given for multiple sizes. The first number refers to the smallest size, and the numbers inside the parentheses refer to the other sizes. Use only the number for the size you want. It helps to photocopy the pattern and highlight only the numbers for your size!

size
Kids S/M (Kids M/L, Adult S/M, Adult M/L)

finished measurements
Circumference around head: 11 (14, 17, 20) inches unstretched
Width: 3 (3, 3½, 3¼) inches unstretched

materials
- 1 skein of Classic Elite Lush [50% wool, 50% angora; 124 yds per 50g skein] (Color used here: 4420)
- 1 12-inch size 5 (3.75mm) circular needle
- 1 cable needle or size 5 (3.75mm) double-pointed needle
- Row counter
- Tapestry needle

tip

To ensure a snug fit, measure around your head and subtract 3–5 inches. This will be your targeted finished size. When in doubt, knit a smaller size as the headband will stretch.

gauge

24 stitches/32 rows = 4 inches in stockinette stitch

pattern

- With a circular needle, cast on 60 (75, 90, 105) stitches. Place stitch marker at start of round. Join to knit in the round, being careful not to twist.
- Work 3 rounds in seed stitch, as follows:
  Round 1: *Knit 1, purl 1* to end of round.
  Round 2: *Purl 1, knit 1* to end of round.
  Round 3: *Knit 1, purl 1* to end of round.
- Next round: *Knit 4, purl 2, knit 2, make 1, knit 3, make 1, knit 2, purl 2* repeat 4 (5, 6, 7) times. You should now have 68 (85, 102, 119) stitches.
- Work rows 1–8 of cable chart 2 times.
- For adult sizes only, repeat rows 1–4 of cable chart one more time.
- For all sizes, next round: *Knit 4, purl 2, knit 2, k2tog, knit 1, k2tog, knit 2, purl 2* repeat 4 (5, 6, 7) times. You should have 60 (75, 90, 105) stitches.
- Repeat rounds 1–3 of seed stitch, as above.
- Bind off all stitches.

cable chart

In the cable chart at right, each box represents a stitch. The row number is given going up the right side of the chart. Cable charts are read from right to left on odd-numbered rows (the public/right side of the knitting), and from left to right on even-numbered rows (the back/wrong side). When you come across a symbol in the chart, follow the directions for that symbol. For example, in row 2, the green symbol means: "Slip 3 stitches to cable needle (or DPN), hold in front of your knitting, knit 3 stitches from the main needle, then knit 3 from the cable needle." After you've done that, you just keep moving across the row, doing knit or purl stitches according to the chart.

finishing

Weave in loose ends, and enjoy!

CABLE CHART

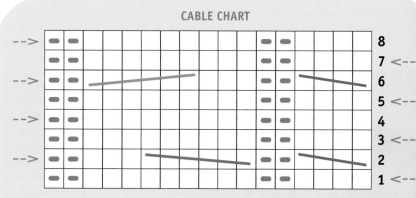

read each row in direction of arrow

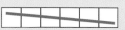
Slip 3 to cable needle, hold in front, knit 3 from main needle, knit 3 from cable needle.

Slip 3 to cable needle, hold in back, knit 3 from main needle, knit 3 from cable needle.

Slip 2 to cable needle, hold in front, knit 2 from main needle, knit 2 from cable needle.

Knit on RS; purl on WS.

Purl on RS; knit on WS.

HOW TO DO THE SEED STITCH

The **seed stitch** is made by knitting one stitch, then moving your yarn between the needles so it's in the front, purling one stitch, moving the yarn to the back, knitting one stitch, and so on until one row or round is completed. On the next row, you knit where you purled, and purl where you knit, forming a checkerboard of knit and purl stitches. It looks fancy, but it's very easy! Try adding rows of seed stitch to the bottom of a hat or scarf.

and STILL more...

9

knitgrrl.com

Whether you need help
or inspiration, it's good
to know where to turn.
You didn't think I'd leave
you hanging, did you?
Happy knitting!

caring for your hand-knit items

Hand-knit items should be washed in cold or slightly warm water with a very mild soap. I use cheap shampoo to wash knitted items, because it's a lot more cost-effective than special detergents and works just as well. If you are washing knits in the sink, do not run water directly onto them (this can cause slight felting). Here's how:

1. Fill the container or sink you're using with cold or room-temperature water. Add the soap or shampoo (not too much!) and swish it around.

2. Add the knitted item and push it under the water to soak. Don't swish it around too much. Leave it to soak for a while. You may want to weight it down with a dinner plate if it keeps floating to the surface. If the water is very soapy after soaking, take the item out and change the water. Don't run fresh water directly onto your knits—you might accidentally felt them a little if the water temperatures are different.

3. Lay out a clean towel on the floor (or on a big table you don't mind getting wet). Lift up the item with both hands, supporting its weight from the bottom (wet wool is stretchy and can easily be pulled out of shape), and place it on the towel.

4. Roll up the towel and step on it a few times to remove as much water from your knit as possible. You may need more towels, depending on the size of the item.

5. Place the now slightly damp item flat on another dry towel (or drying rack) and allow to air dry.

These directions can also be used to wash any kind of wool items. Don't you feel like a laundry genius now? More importantly, if you follow them, you'll never have to worry about shrinking something that took you many hours to make.

tip

Always pick up a wet knitted piece with both hands from the bottom. If you pick up just one side, or one sleeve, it can stretch out of shape.

help! where to get answers (or inspiration)

If it's inspiration you're after, open your eyes to the possibilities of things you already have around you, whether it's yarn scraps someone gave you (hats are great for using up scraps, and so are stripey scarves), or your favorite sweater that doesn't fit you anymore (try unraveling it and knitting the results into something new). When you realize that just about *anything* can be knitted, you'll get some amazing ideas. For example, one time I knitted plastic grocery bags on size 17 needles to make a waterproof shopping bag…maybe next I'll try making a rain poncho with those!

Need more inspiration, or help with a problem? There are plenty of ways to get it—from websites to magazines, and, of course, knitting books.

The companion website to this book (http://www.knitgrrl.com) contains a weblog filled with up-to-the minute news and links, a forum where you can ask questions and post photos of your knitting masterpieces, and much more. If you're having a problem with a particular pattern, chances are you can get an answer directly from me, or the person who designed it.

Knitting-specific magazines and other crafty magazines with knitting content are another way to get ideas. Maybe a beading magazine will inspire a new set of stitch markers, or a fashion magazine will feature scarves with sewn-on felt appliqués and sequins. (You can do that!)

A good knitting library should include at least one book of pattern stitches. Barbara Walker's books are classics, but I also like my *365-day Knitting Pattern* perpetual calendar. I flip through it for ideas to dress up even the plainest patterns. If you keep your abbreviation list handy and follow the directions in order, you can figure out almost any pattern stitch. Remember, all stitch patterns are made up of only two possibilities: knitting and purling. How you use them is up to you!

web

Visit
www.knitgrrl.com
for lots of ideas!

places to go, things to read

H ere is a list of some of my favorite yarn companies, crafty websites, magazines, books, places to buy yarn and supplies online, and organizations to look into.

yarn companies featured in knitgrrl

Brown Sheep: http://www.brownsheep.com

Cascade Yarns: http://www.cascadeyarns.com

Crystal Palace: http://www.straw.com/cpy

Lana Grossa: http://www.lanagrossa.com

Lion Brand: http://www.lionbrand.com

Muench: http://www.muenchyarns.com

online knitting and crafty resources

Knitgrrl: http://www.knitgrrl.com

Knitty: http://www.knitty.com

Knitter's Review: http://www.knittersreview.com

Woolworks: http://www.woolworks.org

Craftster: http://www.craftster.org

Glitter: http://www.supernaturale.com/glitter

Sublime Stitching: http://www.sublimestitching.com

Erica Weiner: http://www.ericaweiner.com

magazines

*knit.*1: http://www.knit1mag.com

Knitter's: http://www.knitters.com

Interweave Knits:
http://www.interweave.com/knits

Vogue Knitting:
http://www.vogueknitting.com

BOOKS

Color Works: The Crafter's Guide to Color, by Deb Menz (Interweave Press, 2004).

Knitting in Plain English, by Maggie Righetti (St. Martin's Press, 1986).

Knitting Without Tears, by Elizabeth Zimmerman (Fireside, 1973).

Stitch-It: Simple Instructions and Tools for 35 Chic to Classic Embroidery Projects, by Jenny Hart (Chronicle Books, 2004).

A Treasury of Knitting Stitches, volumes 1–4, by Barbara Walker (Schoolhouse Press, 1998, 2000).

Vogue Knitting: The Ultimate Knitting Book, by the editors of *Vogue Knitting Magazine* (Sixth&Spring Books, 2002).

Yummy Yarns, by Kathleen and Nick Greco (Watson-Guptill, 2004).

online yarn & supplies

Denise Needles: http://www.knitdenise.com

eBay: http://www.ebay.com

Elann: http://www.elann.com

Jimmy Beans Wool: http://www.jimmybeanswool.com

Patternworks: http://www.patternworks.com

Purl: http://www.purlsoho.com

One Fine Yarn: http://www.onefineyarn.com

Threadbear Fiber Arts:
http://www.threadbearfiberarts.com

There's so much yarn for sale on eBay that it helps to be as specific as possible. Include a brand name, if you can. Searching for "black Cascade wool yarn" will yield much better results than just "yarn."

organizations

Craft Yarn Council of America:
http://www.yarnstandards.com

The Knitter's Guild of America (TKGA):
http://www.tkga.org

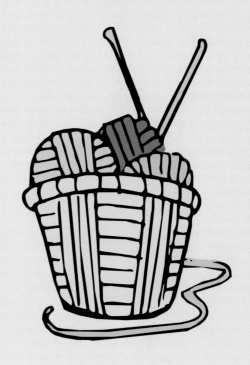

meet the designers

Don't forget, you can "meet" the designers online at http://www.knitgrrl.com. Have a question about a pattern? Why not ask us directly?

Heather Brack (Text-Messaging Mittens, Downtown Messenger Bag) lives in Cleveland, Ohio, with a small dog that will occasionally model scarves for you if asked nicely. She works for a legal publisher and designs her own line of knitting patterns under the name Beeline.

Julie Falatko (Kitty Dim Sum) lives in Maine. She knits when she can, weaves when possible, reads often, and is always looking for an excuse to bake cookies. She also spends time discussing the meaning of life with her husband, caring for her son, petting her cat, and working ever-so-slowly on her librarian degree.

Stacey Irvine (D.I.Y. Leg Warmers) lives in San Francisco, where she knits everything you can think of (and even some things you can't—ever heard of a knitted octopus?).

Stefanie Japel (Music Player Cozy, Soda Cozy) is an American high-pressure geochemist. She knits, lives, and works in Mainz, Germany. She designs almost everything she knits.

Melissa Lim (Faux Fur Stole) lives in Portland, Oregon, where she is an instructional technology teacher. Her mom taught her to knit when she was young, but she didn't start knitting seriously until 1998 when she learned to make her boyfriend a sweater.

Jillian Moreno (Lacy Double-Diamond Scarf) is a totally self-taught designer. She hates rules. She firmly believes that if you obsess on it enough you can do anything. She also believes in excessive chocolate and that girls who knit will grow up to rule the world. She lives in Ann Arbor, Michigan, with her husband, two kids, and way too much yarn.

Gabrielle Peterson (Friendship Scarf) works in scientific publishing when she isn't knitting, and counts the days until she can leave it all behind to knit full time. She lives in Northern California with her husband and daughter.

Amy Swenson (Nakiska Alpine Headband) lives in Calgary, Alberta, with her partner, Sandra, and way too many cats. Her overwhelming addiction to yarn is mostly paid for by her work as a software engineer. Since 2002, she has published her own line of patterns (*IndiKnits*) that can be found in yarn shops across North America.

Shannon Okey (Rocker-Girl Wristlets, Boombox Bag, Stripey Scarf, Ponytail and Heartfelt Roll-Brim Hats), the author of this book, lives in Cleveland, Ohio, with her partner Tamas, her dachshund Anezka, and a very naughty kitten named Spike (see the Kitty Dim Sum pattern—that's him). When she's not knitting or writing, she runs an online store filled with crafty goodness called *anezka handmade* and keeps the knitgrrl.com site running.

index

abbreviations, 17
Acme Knitting Company, 80

binding off, 27
blocking, 77
Boombox Bag, 36–38
Brack, Heather, 70–72, 78–79, 95

cable crossing, 85
cable needles, 85
cables, 85
carrying the yarn, 65
casting on, 20–21
circular needles, 14
    working with, 53
color
    knitting with more than one, 64–65
yarn, choosing right, 12–13
cozy
    Music Player, 66–68
    Soda, 69
Craft Yarn Council of America, 9, 94
crochet hooks, 15

Denise Needles, 15, 31, 94
D.I.Y. Leg Warmers, 58–60
double-pointed needles (DPNs), 14
    how to use, 63
double yarn over (YO2), 81
Downtown Messenger Bag, 78–79
dropping a stitch, 29
duplicate stitch, 86

embroidery, 86

Fair Isle, 64–65, 72
Falatko, Julie, 48–50, 95
Faux Fur Stole, 46–47
felting, 75
    and shrinkage, 79
float, 65
Friendship Scarf, 34–35

garter stitch, 25
gauge, measuring, 30
grafting, 28

hand-knit items, care of, 91
Hart, Jenny, 87
Headband, Nakiska Alpine, 88–89
Heartfelt Roll-Brim Hat, 56–57

i-cord, 84
intarsia, 64–65
    -style patterning, 72
Irvine, Stacey, 58–60, 95

Japel, Stefanie, 66–68, 69, 95

Kitty Dim Sum, 48–50
    egg roll, 50
    wonton, 49
knit 2 together (k2tog), 43, 47
knit 2 together through back loop (k2tog tbl), 44, 47
knit fabric, creating, 25
knit stitch, 22–23
    combining purl stitch and, 25
knit through front and back loop (k1fb), 42, 47
knitting
    abbreviations, 17, 47
    binding off, 27
    books and magazines, 93
    celebrities who do it, 7
    and crafty resources, online, 93
    getting answers or inspiration for, 92
    with more than one color, 64–65
    organizations, 94
    party, hosting, 39
    reasons for, 6–7
    in the round, 53
    salve for rough hands, making your own, 73
    starting first row of, 20–21

stitches, 22–24
    tools, 15
knitting needles, 14–15, 19, 85
    how to use double-pointed, 63
    working with circular, 53

lace, basics of, 80–81
Lacy Double-Diamond Scarf, 80–81
Leg Warmers, D.I.Y., 58–60
Lim, Melissa, 46–47, 95
local yarn store (LYS), 7

make 1 (m 1), 41
Mittens, Text-Messaging, 70–72
Moreno, Jillian, 80–81, 95
Music Player Cozy, 66–68

Nakiska Alpine Headband, 88–89
needles, 14–15, 85
    See also knitting needles
    for swatching, 31
    and yarn, holding, 19

Okey, Shannon, 33, 36–38, 51, 54–55, 56–57, 95

patterns, reading, 16
Peterson, Gabrielle, 34–35, 95
picture knitting, 64–65
pom-poms, 83
Ponytail Roll-Brim Hat, 54–55
purl 2 together (p2tog), 44
purl stitch, 24
    combining knit stitch and, 25

reverse stockinette, 25
Rocker-Girl Wristlets, 33
roll-brim hat
    Heartfelt, 56–57
    Ponytail, 54–55
row counter, 15
scarf
    Lacy Double-Diamond, 80–81
    Stripey, 51
seaming, 28

seed stitch, 89
slip, slip, knit (SSK), 45
Soda Cozy, 69
stitches, 22–25
    accidentally adding or dropping, 29
    adding, 41–42
    duplicate, 86
    picking up stitches at bottom edge of already-knit, 76
    seed, 89
    ways to decrease, 43–45
    ways to increase, 41–42
stitch holders, 15
    using, 35
stitch markers, 15
    how to use, 55
    making your own, 61
stockinette, 25, 57
straight needles, 14
Stripey Scarf, 51
Sublime Stitching, 87
swatches, 30–31
Swenson, Amy, 88–89, 95

tapestry needles, 15, 28
Text-Messaging Mittens, 70–72

weaving in ends, 28
Weiner, Erica, 51, 93

yarn
    choosing colors for, 12–13
    companies, 93
    facts to know about, 9
    holding needles and, 19
    joining new, 26
    labels, reading, 10
    quiz for choosing right, 11
    and supplies, online, 94
    weight system, Craft Yarn Council of America's standard, 9
yarn float, 65
yarn needles, 15
yarn over (YO), 29
    how to do, 81